I CAME OUT SIDEWAYS

I CAME OUT SIDEWAYS

From Liverpool to Another Place

George Porter

CHAPLIN BOOKS

www.chaplinbooks.co.uk

ISBN 978-1-909183-67-4

A CIP catalogue record for this book is available from The British
Library.

Design by Michael Walsh at The Better Book Company
Printed by Imprint Digital

Chaplin Books
1 Eliza Place
Gosport PO12 4UN
Tel: 023 9252 9020
www.chaplinbooks.co.uk

CONTENTS

For Paul Berry, a decent man who could make
himself heard without ever raising his voice.

1

THE FAULT LINE

I came out sideways. Neither head nor bottom first, but sideways. This unusual and distressing exit from the warmth, comfort and security of the womb was conducted by the composer himself – The Führer. There must be a grain of truth about my admission to the world, for my sideways entry seemed to permeate my being and give me a distorted understanding of everything that surrounded me.

Not that I recall any of Hitler's atrocious melodies played on the day of my birth, though in my early childhood, I could see the evidence of them. In my fresh and unsullied eyes, the blasted skeletons of buildings and the wastelands of demolition that went with them were not scenes of devastation, ruin and shambles, but were playgrounds as common and as exciting as any country garden would have been to a child of a noble. I didn't know that I was deprived. I didn't know I was sickly. Pneumonia was something I 'got'. Coats doubled as blankets, and newspaper doubled as toilet paper. A jam butty was ambrosia, and scouse was cuisine of the most superior kind. Tripe was the pits. Nothing to me was more sumptuously satisfying than a large viscous splodge of Fussell's condensed milk spread on a wedge of fresh bread. I was, in the eyes of my childhood contemporaries, normal. And it was, until the age of about eleven, a pleasant existence.

In reality we were neither poor nor deprived in the conventional sense. We lived on the cusp; a fault-line between material wellbeing on one side and grating poverty on the other, and, undoubtedly because of my father's proclivity for backing losing horses, we had a foot in both camps. For some of our neighbours, Waterloo was just a step away from the terrors of the Liverpool slums and the wastelands of the blitzkrieg, but for most of us, including me, it was a very agreeable place to live.

It is set on a bank of the River Mersey about three miles from the famous Gladstone Dock. Before a marina was built in the 1970s for the few locals who owned yachts, it had an endless beach of fine sand and dunes, stretching as far as you could see past Formby Point and on to the northern Mecca of Blackpool Tower, a jagged black speck in the far distance. Across the river once stood a less celebrated, but even taller, tower at 577 feet, that of New Brighton, and if the eye travelled further the lower slopes of the mountains of North Wales became evident. Great ocean liners and merchant ships from around the globe sauntered up and down the River Mersey, displaying their shipping lines by the coloured stripes and stars on their funnels. Old sea dogs would sit up against the beach wall with their binoculars continuously trained out to sea, muttering to each other in a nasal Liverpool patois about which was what ship and who had sailed on her and where she had come from and where she was going and what she carried and, and, and …

On Sundays in the summer, families from the shattered remnants of Scotland Road and Bootle day-tripped the four stops to Waterloo by rail on the Liverpool-to-Southport line and walked en masse past the Victorian and Edwardian parade of shops in South Road to the shore, bellicose and bawdy, displaying their rough but sometimes gentle self-effacing humour which is the worldwide trademark perpetually boasted of by the Scouser to the Scouser. They'd stop at the Golden Goose and Mr de Roose's corner shop to buy ice-cream, candy floss, buckets-and-spades, and little plastic windmills on sticks, taking a day off from the harsh hand dealt them by a war they had been told they had won. Then it was off down the slope onto the beach or into the sand dunes for games of hide-and-seek or more adult activities. Sometimes an enormous box kite could be seen flying high in the sky, dwarfing the smaller diamond-shaped ones pulled along by whooping small boys. Trenches were dug in the damp sand alongside the concrete dragons' teeth tank-traps intended to hamper the German tanks which never arrived, and into those trenches jumped dirty-faced imaginary soldiers in their ragged underpants, some with pop guns, most with plastic pistols.

Who would have believed that in half a century these tank-traps would be replaced by the poignant statues deposited at random by

Anthony Gormley, all gazing out to sea towards another place? Little girls scraped hopscotch frames in the very sand where one day the metal feet of those figures would be planted.

The girls spent their time jumping from one square to another, or doing handstands with their dresses firmly secured in the legs of their knickers. Other children undertook the laborious task of trying to dig through to Australia, and some even risked disease or getting stuck in the mud by paddling in the Mersey. I was warned about getting a disease, but never got one, although I did get stuck once when the tide was out. A tall man, up to his knees in the mud, pulled me out – yowling – with a plop. The shore was heaven on earth for a day for people worn down but not out, existing in the darkness cloaking the half-truth of England's green and pleasant land, known of but never seen by most of those children whose fathers had fought for it. Many of those fathers never came home and many who did, returned to a devastated wasteland of mangled masonry and craters where houses once stood. Bootle had only 15 percent of its houses left undamaged after the war, and that is how we finished up living in Waterloo.

The room into which I was shoehorned by Dr Novak, who oversaw my cumbersome arrival and attended to later sicknesses with gentle concern, was the bedroom of a decaying Victorian flat above a builder's office. I can still recall an image of the doctor warming the business end of his stethoscope against his arm before applying it to my wheezing chest. We all shared one bedroom, my older brother and my parents, and when my cot became too small for me, a second single bed was acquired and strapped on top of another to form a rickety and precarious nest for my brother on the upper level, with a roomy little house for me below. In fact the structure was roomier than the rest of the floor-space available to us all. The windows rattled, the rain ran down the walls inside, and the oilcloth lifted off the floor whenever a gust of wind blew in. Slates were missing from the roof and bowls and pots were strategically placed to catch the downpours from the ceiling. On a cold, wet and windy day I would awaken not to the clunk, clunk, clunk, clunk clatter of the shunting goods trains in the sidings opposite our home, but to rattling windows and the slushy hypnotic swish of the waves of the

River Mersey gliding onto the beach some two hundred yards away, accompanied by the squawks of seagulls bickering over scraps.

Next to the bedroom was a slightly larger room which we called the kitchen. This caused confusion in my mind as I grew up, for similar – although more luxurious – rooms in the more conventional houses of the children I later became acquainted with were known as 'living' or 'sitting' rooms. Our cooking was done in the 'back kitchen', which did make some sense, for indeed it was situated at the back. This kitchen was shared with my maternal grandmother, Martha, a cross between Old Mother Riley and Queen Mary, who occupied the greater part of two floors of the precarious rotting structure of number four, Church Road. In one corner of the 'back kitchen' was a big old Edwardian coal-fired range which was her divine right and was only used for the cooking of tripe, and in the other corner an ancient gas cooker on which my scouse, porridge, and eggs were cooked by my mother.

My grandmother, the only grandparent I knew, was – and is still – an enigma to me. I have only a few vivid memories of any communication I had with her. One was when she told my friend Albert that he couldn't come into our house with a dirty face – he ran away crying. Another was scaring me witless by telling me, as she dragged me into the butcher's shop on South Road for her weekly portion of tripe, that the butcher would chop off my fingers and make them into sausages. This terrifying threat was given even greater credence by the butcher himself, who aided Martha in the subterfuge by frowning at me through his bushy eyebrows while honing his big knife.

I recollect her making me stand on a chair in her room next door to ours, which was usually off limits, and conduct while she sang *We're Soldiers of the Queen, My Boys*. At Church Road, she had a large room to herself where she would lie in silent stately repose on an ancient threadbare chaise longue. She would boil her soot-blackened kettle on a moving iron griddle over the mean little fire she assembled for herself every day. Her lighting was supplied by ancient gas lamps on hinges attached to the wall – in 1890 they would have been very contemporary. She always had coal, but she retained it under lock and key in a shed in the back yard. We often seemed to run out of coal, although Martha's copper scuttle was always full. We made do with a battered old galvanised bucket. She had a piano which was also locked and never, ever, played. I was led to believe that it was a repository for bundles of large white five-pound notes. She was a miser, although the fear of dying in the Liverpool workhouse where she was thought to have been resident at one time, was most likely entrenched in her psyche.

One day a big policeman came to our house to see Martha. It emerged that she had lost her purse somewhere on South Road and it had been handed in at the police station. It contained some of these five-pound notes, and the policeman was interested in how such a large amount of money had found its way into the purse of a very old lady living in what could quite rightly be described as reduced circumstances. He left after a short time, bewildered.

The answer to the locked and unplayed piano could lie in the auspicious circumstances of the death of Martha's husband, a Scottish marine engineer. Several confusing myths grew up around him, one being that he had been torpedoed; another was that he'd been a chief engineer on board the *Mauretania*, sister liner of the *Lusitania*, where a hatch had fallen on him and he'd lost an eye. A much more audacious anecdote was that he had tested the water on board the ship, but it had been poisoned by the Turks and he had died as a consequence and been buried in Alexandria. This was the source of the wads of five-pound notes believed to be secreted in the piano. He had had a glass eye and a red beard. These are two indisputable facts, because my brother knew where the glass eye was kept. There was also a spare, and there were occasions when a clandestine game of marbles was played. I inherited the red beard and also the stout proportions.

Up two further flights of stairs was my grandmother's bedroom – a place I never recall visiting until after she had died. It later became our bedroom and to me it was always imbued with an aroma of peppermints, as if she sometimes dawdled around the room in my fearful mind's eye, shuffling across the floor in the middle of the night. This additional room for me and my brother enabled my parents to have a measure of peace and privacy, and for us to have more space for serious combat. Next to her bedroom was a treasure house. Contained in this gloomy Dickensian chamber, which we called 'the attic', with its broken and cracked fanlight, paper curling off dripping walls, ancient plaster dropping in lumps and the pervading smell of damp distemper and rotting wood, was where my grandfather's collection of possessions transported home from his voyages was stored. Who would believe that so many treasures were stowed away in such a place? There were several exquisitely carved and beautifully embellished wooden spears, pristine as the day they had been carved. Leaning up against the wall were two enormous turtle shells polished to such a sheen that I could see my face reflected in them, and a box containing assorted wooden carvings and ornaments. Some native drums were enclosed in this tomb, never to beat out the pulsating rhythms intended, or to be at the heart of a tribal ritual.

Fact, however – as we know – can sometimes be even more enthralling than fiction, and the authenticity of the myths which grew up around him is much more fascinating than the half-truths I came to know. A ship he sailed on as the second engineer, HMHS *Lanfranc*, was indeed torpedoed in the Channel, conveying British and German wounded from Normandy, and now sits almost intact on the seabed. My grandfather wasn't on board, however, because he had died a year earlier on this same ship transporting the wounded to Alexandria from the Dardanelles. He wasn't buried in Alexandria; he was buried *at sea* off Alexandria with full military honours, although a merchant seaman, because he had indeed tested the drinking water and was said to have died of dysentery and there is evidence that the water supply at the time had been tainted by the Turks. It was reported in the Australian press, although not in the British press – Churchill had seen to that.

Prior to World War I, the *Lanfranc* sailed regularly a thousand miles up the Amazon to Manaus through jungle and rainforest. Hence the turtle shells which originated from the region. These were the shells of the largest freshwater turtle in the world, and the 'spears' were not spears at all, but ceremonial paddles, examples of which I later saw in the British Museum.

My paternal grandfather, Joseph, is buried in the ancient Norman church of St Helen, Sefton, which dates from 1111, the inside walls of which display plaques commemorating some of my uncles who were killed in the trenches to be remembered alongside crusader knights on the same walls. He had left my father's multifarious brothers and sisters – ten, I was told, but am not sure – not for another woman, but for another pint of Guinness. I was told he was an Irish immigrant, and also an Orangeman replete with all the prejudices inherent in the extreme version of this phenomenon: it was said that the only flowers he would grow were orange lilies. He cycled into the Leeds and Liverpool Canal one night on his way home from the tannery where he worked. The story has it that he had a bottle of Guinness in each of his overcoat pockets when both he and his bicycle were recovered from the canal. My father was only five years old when this occurred. Joseph's wife, Elizabeth, died some short time later and is buried with my grandfather. I was told she died of a broken heart, but I think it was more likely that she died from the stress and strain of an unending quest to feed so many mouths with so little support. Thereafter, it was my father's born-blind sister Alice – the oldest of them – who reputedly became the head of the family.

My mother fretted constantly, cried often, had 'nerves' and consumed large quantities of Beecham's Pills, along with anti-depressant tablets supplied in bulk by the caring Dr Novak. Money was her constant concern, not because my father didn't work but because he gambled most of his wages on horses. The horses with which he was financially acquainted were either 'bloody crabs', 'beaten by a bloody nostril', or sometimes a nose hair. He literally gambled it all away, what little there was. One incident which comes to mind is the shame and humiliation I suffered when I was made to carry, on a borrowed handcart, my mother's only prized possession – a large sewing machine – to a secondhand shop called Rosie's which boasted a huge supply of debris deposited by neighbours for a few coppers so they could supplement a dwindling supply of coal from the railway sidings opposite with cheap briquettes of compressed coal-dust. I believe Rosie had a financial interest in the production of this combustible shite, so that many of the coppers she doled out to the financially strapped clientele of her little empire of rags travelled full circle into the greasy bulging pockets of her tattered Royal Navy greatcoat replete with the corroded insignia of a naval officer. My mother had a wedding ring, but her engagement ring had gone on a similar journey to a pawnbroker's window prior to my birth and never been retrieved.

The grief of tears.
The twisted anguish in a piece of cloth
Which stems the flow of rivers of woe
Showing all to plain
The ache of living

My mother had a friend called Doris Leatherbarrow whose facial arrangement was assembled as if it had been carved out of the same material as her surname and who delivered omens displayed in tea-leaves, which seemed to do nothing except intensify my mother's manifold anxieties. I can still see Doris Leatherbarrow now when my mind is idling in neutral. She had a Roman nose, non-existent eyebrows, sunken cheeks coated with scarlet blusher, pink hair and an unnerving and malevolent piercing cackle which seemed to occur whenever there was a hiatus in the conversation. When she shook her head, as she often did when viciously slating her husband, a cloud of Woolworth's scented face powder would be discharged. Her pink hair was tightly curled into her head, displaying rivers of white skin winding paths through her skull in the aftermath of her removed metal hair grips. She wore a bottle-green gabardine coat, never removed, buttoned up to the neck, regardless of the temperature. When she pursed her painted lips they would crack and morph into a cat's business end. Her voice had the hard edge to it of one who cared not for the niceties of polite refined conversation, although when she drank her tea she did so with the exaggerated demeanour of a dowager taking tiffin, holding her cup between her scarlet-tipped forefinger and thumb, with her little finger poking out horizontally to the saucer balanced dexterously in her left hand.

Conversation usually centred on her much-maligned husband, a man my mother had never met but who was vilified to such an extent that, when eavesdropping from under the table while hammering small nails into the wooden underframe of my little tricycle with my toy hammer, even at such a tender age I would have been able to stand up in court and give evidence relating to the beast she married in haste without prior knowledge of what sort of a useless bone-idle article he was. On the subject of the climate, in later life she became convinced, being of a paranormal disposition, that all our bad weather was a result of the Sputnik after the satellite was launched and she cursed the Russians for the rain.

> *"Oo Jean, I can tell yer 'dis – 'ee's such an idle bugger dat 'ee sleeps with 'is bloody socks on. Too bloody lazy to take them off. I'll tell yer dis – If 'ee carries on da way 'ees goin', I'LL put a bloody sock in 'IM! Eee makes your George look like bloody Superman."*

I don't think Mrs Leatherbarrow had ever set eyes on my father, for if she had, her description would not have stood up to scrutiny. He had a pigeon chest, and every vein in both of his legs was varicose. He suffered from chronic pleurisy as a result of smoking twenty Woodbines every day along with a half-ounce of St Bruno tobacco for his pipe at weekends.

The reading of the tea-leaves usually took place after her offensive ranting regarding the uselessness of Mr Leatherbarrow, and after complimenting me on my skills with a small hammer and nails and my new-found ability to wipe my own bottom, a function she had personally supervised on several occasions when I was caught short, while my mother was busily involved in making the tea and recovering the custard creams she thought were hidden from me alongside the sweetened condensed milk under the cupboard in the back kitchen, in readiness of the psychobabble she was about to be subjected to.

> *"Oo, 'ee's a good lad dat Georgie, isn't 'ee. 'Ee's a little smasher dat one isn't 'ee? I'll tell yer dis, Jean, dat one's goin' ta break a few hearts when 'ee grows up. They'd better lock up their daughters when 'ee's around."*

The tea-leaves ceremony always seemed to culminate with my mother in a more extreme condition of nervous debilitation than when Doris Leatherbarrow had appeared as if spirited into the house. She never knocked on our front door; she must have crept up the normally creaking stairs in order to make a mystically theatrical entrance as if to bolster her claim to psychic powers. She was able to enter our house with such covert silence because she was aware that the door key was suspended from a length of string on the inside of the door underneath the letterbox. Her speculative deception was that of a clairvoyant. She clarified the various disturbing implications revealed in the little mounds of spent tea leaves contained in the bottom of teacups. She would turn a lipstick-ringed cup upsidedown in a saucer with an exaggerated twist of her wrists, and drain away the residue of liquid in the bottom of it, close her eyes and mutter a few inaudible words, turn it up the correct way in slow motion and then peer into it through glazed red-crazed eyes. Then she would pontificate.

"Oo Jean, I can see an 'orse again. Not da same one, mind. Dis one's got longer legs. Can you see it? And look, der's a man on da ground. 'Ee's fallen off it! Look, look, can you see it? And just look at dat fence – da 'orse 'as run right through it!"

Even at the age of four, I was aware that this woman was a charlatan. She was as well aware as I was regarding the hazardous condition of our finances due to my father's unremitting ruinous investment in the turf, for when a really bad day of racing investment had taken place I would hear the raised voices of my parents quarrelling well into the night, culminating in sobs of despair and anguish from my mother.

Regardless of her dissolute chicanery, a still-unexplained phenomenon occurred some thirteen years later regarding Doris Leatherbarrow, when she was still appearing in a puff of Woolworth's powder – terrifying both the cat and my mother – just in time for a cup of tea. Her alleged remarkable powers of delving into the mysteries of the unknown went into overdrive one day when she saw me walking down the stairs and called out to me. I was wearing, she said, pale blue drainpipe trousers, bronze winkle-pickers with Cuban heels and a scarlet shirt. I had completely ignored her. Unknown to her, when she hailed me on the stairs, I was actually several hundred miles away in Germany serving as a young soldier, having a further operation related to a broken arm, the splintering of which had become a regular habit. There was a problem encountered in attempting to bring me round from the anaesthetic and I was unable to be revived for about an hour. It was during this period that I was supposed to have been seen by Doris Leatherbarrow walking down the stairs. Mrs Leatherbarrow was so convinced she'd seen me that my mother, already in a nervous panic, telephoned the army to check that I had not deserted, *"because if he has, please don't put him in prison because he's a good boy really"*. The military machine sprang into action and located my whereabouts, informing my mother that I was in hospital and I should have let her know of this; therefore, I would be disciplined at a later stage, which I was. Two weeks confined to barracks. All this further aggravated my mother's nerves, nearly sending her over the edge and resulting in the fracturing of relations with the lunatic who had for many years drained my quota of custard creams.

No-one could believe this nonsense, except that prior to the rupturing of relations with my mother, Doris Leatherbarrow described to her the clothes I was wearing when she allegedly saw me on the stairs. I should have been in uniform when admitted to the military hospital, but was excused from wearing it because it was the weekend, and therefore I was off duty. I had bought my entire outfit, from the drainpipe trousers to the winkle-pickers, in Germany and had never worn those clothes in England, yet she described them, or so I was told, in detail.

No doubt my sideways entrance to the world would have been manna from heaven to aid the portentous ramblings of Mrs Leatherbarrow had she known of it. I can just imagine it:

> *"Oo, Jean! That's why 'ee keeps breaking 'is arm and walking backwards. I think 'ee's being guided along a different path than us."*

Perhaps she did know about my sideways entrance into the world. For many years I wondered whether this crone had in fact put a spell on me, and even now I sometimes shudder at the thought that I may have spent my life wandering down a pre-ordained path locked in a force-field emanating from her secreted psyche. We don't keep any biscuits in our house, and tea bags negate the anxiety associated with the thought of surreptitiously probing the innards of a tea cup for signs of sideways inclinations.

2

ALFIE – THE SEVEN-YEAR-OLD GYNAECOLOGIST

I am sitting shivering on the lavatory. No coal, no warmth. Frost and draughts. My father is standing at the chipped crazed basin lathering his face with a ragged shaving brush that has seen better days and he is singing *I Dream of Jeannie with the Light Brown Hair* in his rich baritone voice which, when he was a boy soprano at Sefton, had once graced the towering arches of Liverpool Cathedral in front of King George V. His aquiline reflection serenades him from the fogged, cracked, ancient mirror above the freezing taps. Steam spirals up from the dented tin kettle perched on the edge of the battleship-grey crusty bath – a spacious affair which at its zenith would have been the pride of a privileged family, but had since become a forlorn and decaying manifestation of past affluence.

"Dad." No reply.

"DAD!

"You silly little sod! I'm trying to shave. I'll cut my bloody throat if you shout like that. What do you want? If it's your bottom you want wiping, you're big enough to do it yourself."

"Dad – where do I come from?"

"Bloody Liverpool, that's where you come from. Now get on with you bloody business and don't be so bloody daft."

"Dad – who made me?"

"Ask your mother."

> *"She told me to ask you. Anyway, I know 'cos Aflie*
> *Littlehales told me."*
>
> *"What do you mean, you know?"*
>
> *"Alfie Littlehales said you made me with your tommie*
> *by putting it in mum."*
>
> *"Now I HAVE cut myself. Look what you have made*
> *me do, you silly little sod. Get out of here and leave*
> *me alone or I'll take my belt to you. And don't let me*
> *catch you with that dirty little nomark or you will feel*
> *the back of my hand!"*

The threats were empty threats. For all the bluster he never raised a finger to me, save for the day when – again under the influence of my guide and mentor through my early childhood, the nomark Alfie Littlehales – I boldly leapt in front of a hearse carrying a corpse on its journey to the fires of oblivion. It was a typical game of 'chicken' we were engaged in, but unbeknown to me the driver of the hearse was my father. The cortège came to an unscheduled and undignified standstill on the corner of Church Road and Wesley Street. Out from the driver's seat jumped an extremely angry man while I stood mortified, rooted to the spot like a rabbit trapped in bright headlights. Alfie, on the other hand, was away down the road at an ass's gallop. As I said, until that day my father had never raised a finger to me, and even at that juncture it was his foot that just scraped my rear end as I regained sensibility and ran. When I arrived home I didn't mention the event to my mother but mooched about the room for the remainder of the day in a haze of apprehensive foreboding.

> *"Do you know what this little bugger's been up to,*
> *Jean? He's taken to jumping in front of bloody cars.*
> *Not just any old car, but bloody funeral cars. Not*
> *just any bloody funeral car, but the one I am driving*
> *loaded up with a bloody body! If I catch him with that*
> *little nomark again, I'll take the bloody skin off his*
> *backside."*

And that was it. As usual, he didn't take his belt off to thrash me as was normally threatened in situations of a similar nature, but I made myself scarce nonetheless.

The undertaker my father worked for lied to me that he kept a turkey behind his office door to gobble up naughty boys. He wore a black bowler hat and a button-popping waistcoat with a gold watch and chain and pin-striped trousers. He was a spherical little person of the W C Fields variety who rolled when he walked. When I first met him I didn't know what an undertaker was. I assumed that he undertook to do things for people and made boxes for them. In a sense I was correct. Outside his little office, on one side were housed the big black limousines which my father maintained and drove, and on the other side was the box-making department. The unique blend of oil, petrol, varnish and sawdust is an aroma which still lives with me.

The undertaker's wife was a buxom woman who towered over him. She wore an enormous black fur coat with a matching hat rather like a cooking pot without a handle. The shoulders of the coat were so wide that she had to enter the office sideways. One day she grabbed me and kissed me on the cheek, leaving a big red damp smudge on the side of my face. It was she who informed me that there was no turkey behind the office door, and the noises I heard coming from his office were sounds made by the undertaker himself to keep me out of his office because he did not want my sticky little fingers on his typewriter keys, or the machine clogging with chewing gum. Also, there was the issue of the disappearing typing paper and pencils.

His office, garage and workshop were ideally situated for his profession, for it was opposite the back-to-back infested dwellings of Chapel Street, a street I never set foot in for fear of becoming a victim of a disease called diphtheria and dying, or so I was told on numerous occasions. Also close by was the mortuary, which had served his business well during the recent war years. When I was a little older, I would scale the outside wall after business hours, in the morbid hope that someone had left the odd corpse lying around. I sometimes played with the children I knew from this area but I was aware that they lived a harder, more brutal, existence than me. I was sometimes called a 'proddy dog', not knowing that this was a Catholic abusive expression for a Protestant. Nevertheless, we rubbed along in a guarded fashion.

*

There was a little boy who used to come and visit his grandmother at the bottom of the mean cobbled street next to our house. It was near a bomb-site and an air-raid shelter which had been reborn as the unofficial headquarters of a motley assortment of the children of seamen, dockers and labourers. There they would 'play', and one of their favourite games was tormenting this little boy whose name I do not recall, but whose sad little pinched face is etched bold in my memory.

He looked much like his contemporaries, but at an early stage in life I learned that appearances can deceive, for this little boy was unable to speak. He would wring his hands and contort his face but the only sounds that he was able to produce were whining noises interspersed with grunts. The more excited he became, the more frequent the grunts tumbled from his lips.

However, the games he assumed he was playing were sport for others. A sport more entertaining than squashing frogs, pissing in letterboxes, or even dancing around swearing and spitting at old mad May, a poor demented soul. She manifested all the physical signs of a troubled and disturbed mind. Her hair was arranged in an institutionalised fashion, cropped just below the neck with no attempt at styling and her sad but watchful eyes were constantly darting about bird-like on the lookout for imagined and sometimes real attacks on her person. She wore a long grey raincoat which trailed at her feet and she muttered incoherently as she shuffled along the street in her carpet slippers. At least she could shout at her tormentors. As for their supposed playmate, there was no fear of reprisals. They could poke him, pull his ears, kick him, pinch him and much, much worse. Speech came from his eyes, for his mouth was merely an opening for food, and the words that tumbled hotly down his crinkly little cheeks said, or so I believed, "Please don't – I want to be friends."

After an hour or so, his sister would come out into the street to take him home, and she would mistake the words pouring out of his eyes for common tears. She would tell his tormentors in the guise of playmates that he was tired and that it was time for him to go home. As he toddled off up the street clutching his sister with his tiny hand, unable to discharge the belly-sized sob held inside him, the assumed friends of this little boy would snigger.

Later in my bed, I would cry common tears, not words, and ask God why the little boy could not talk. I never received a reply.

*

Alfie Littlehales was a string bean of a child, of the species which grew up after a war he had never experienced, but which made him what he was – rickety, malnourished, myopic and very spotty. Also he tended to accumulate boils on the back of his neck. Because the stark facts of his circumstances were neither known – nor cared for – by him, he was living, breathing evidence that regardless of what obstacles life can throw at some of us, our lives are not meaningless; nor need they be dismal and cast by worry. He whistled. Incessantly and discordantly. He emanated a peculiar odour of stale biscuits. His NHS spectacles with their pink-encased wire rims always seemed not quite to fit, and thus he was prone to jerk his head spasmodically sideways, to get them to slip back into position. His thin legs were slightly cabriole and his feet, which were rather large in contrast to the rest of his build, were made even more prominent by the addition of a pair of heavily scuffed boots which were several sizes too large for him. They were scuffed to the extent that the black leather on the toe end revealed patches of a grey fuzzy substance that resembled cardboard more than leather. He kicked everything – tin cans, bottles, stones, cigarette packets and anything else in the road that was kickable. These boots had metal rims on the soles at the toe end and at the heel, and if he scraped his heel hard on the pavement he could make sparks fly, a trick he performed regularly for me. The backs of these boots were also ruthlessly scuffed as a result of many idle hours spent sitting on a wall swinging his legs backwards and forwards against it. I was jealous of his boots. They were manufactured to be indestructible and to give lifelong service regardless of the size of the feet of their occupants. They were boots designed for the poorer sections of the community and were considered to be one up from the lowest caste – that of those who wore no footwear, like Joey Dewsbury who once tried to kill me because I was a Protestant, or at least that is what he was telling me when he was throttling me on the ground. My mother used to threaten me with imprisonment in a pair of these supposedly imperishable boots if I didn't stop scuffing the toes of my brother's oversized and scuff-free cast-offs, although I knew even then that I would never be so fortunate as to own a pair of them, for pride was redolent – regardless of the lack of finances due to jockeys falling off horses and blind horses running into fences.

I was walking on the big field when I met Alfie kicking broken bricks and throwing a chair leg for Spike, a local terrier of unknown provenance. The field wasn't really very big and wasn't really a field. It was a lumpy patch of wasteland and broken bricks, with rough hillocks of grass growing over the remnants of what once had been buildings. Some outside walls were left still intact despite the Luftwaffe's futile attempts to flatten Liverpool and were ideal training areas for practising climbing garden walls. Spike the dog, however, was not interested in the chair leg. He had caught the attention of a saucy little female who was playfully dancing around him. Off they went across the big field on a journey of desire and sociable exhilaration. We followed at a leisurely pace; I was oblivious to what was to be the outcome of this peculiar behaviour by Spike, who was usually only too happy to retrieve chair legs. Alfie, on the other hand, seemed to be in possession of some clandestine intimate knowledge regarding Spike's perplexing and irrational conduct. Eventually we encountered the two dogs in the middle Church Road about thirty yards from my home. They were adhered together. I was puzzled and a little unnerved at the sight, but Alfie seemed shrewdly nonchalant.

> *"What are they doing?"*
> *"Der 'avin a shag."*
> *"What's a shag?"*
> *"It's what yer dad does with yer mam to make babies.*
> *It's how dey made yew. He puts his dick in her fanny*

and plants a seed in her."

"What's a fanny?"

*"It's what wimmin 'av instead of dicks. Dey doesn't 'av
dicks like us. Da seed grows inside until it's a baby
and den it pops out through 'er fanny."*

I was naturally both perturbed and confused by this outrageous
and disturbing gem of gynaecological information delivered with
such an air of knowledgeable authority by my sage. I questioned
him further to enable me to digest this implausible bombshell. The
information conveyed to me by Alfie, which I enthusiastically
disclosed to my father while 'doing my business', was the cause
of his departure from the house that morning with a bleeding chin
sparsely masked by small scraps of paper torn from the *Crosby
Herald*, an issue of which had once displayed a front-page picture
of a children's party with me sitting cross-legged on the floor in
the centre of the group, sticking my tongue out. The editor of this
popular local newspaper would go to his grave oblivious to the grief
he brought to bear on the day that a copy arrived at 4 Church Road.

We stood watching the display of canine lasciviousness, me with
a certain degree of anxiety, and Alfie with a shrewd expression on his
knowledgeable countenance while Spike, wallowing in the throes of
extreme ecstasy, seemed unaware of our presence. I was in awe of
such a spectacle, wondering if that was really how babies were made,
or if Alfie had been purposely misinformed by his elder siblings.

Mrs Evans, a porcine lady of gargantuan proportions, whose
son Arthur once gave me a bloody nose in return for a black eye,
lurched onto the scene, shod in her well-corroded carpet slippers
with stockings rolled down to her bulging, blubbery ankles and
a colourful headdress suggestive of a tea-towel covering the hair
curlers swinging at will from her perspiring temple. To complete this
disagreeable vision, she bulged threateningly out of a large flowery-
patterned stained and crumpled cross-over apron which battled
courageously to restrain the upper half of her torso from bursting
forth in a mountain of unbridled flab. Her legs were dappled with
red marks as a result of sitting too near to a fire in an otherwise cold
room for extended periods of inactivity. She had the omnipresent

Woodbine stuck to her trembling lower lip and her mouth was agape, displaying blackened teeth and several gaps where others had once resided. My father said she had a bloody face fit to frighten the bloody horses. The horses he was associated with unquestionably needed frightening. She certainly terrified me. She was lugging a buckled, galvanised bucket of water with her that she let fly at the dogs, but as a result of the bucket's bent handle, not only did the dogs get a drenching but she took the severity of an after-shock of the residue from the bucket directly in her face. The cigarette sagged, but miraculously remained secured to her lip. She wobbled to a halt, the shock-waves proceeding up her body until their mounting crescendo reached her head and burst forth in an agonised wail.

"You DIRTY little buggers!"

I didn't know whether the abuse was directed at us, the dogs, or all four of us, but we scattered in different directions, me to the relative safety of 4 Church Road. Relative safety only, because there had been a recent doorstep event involving Mrs Evans and my mother regarding an alleged kick to the ankle directed forcefully by me when she was apparently dragging me off Arthur who was, according to her, about to be murdered. Mrs Evans produced the evidence in the form of a large blue bruise which complimented and blended appealingly with the mottled redness surrounding it. My mother informed Mrs Evans in strident colloquial terms that her son was a good boy and would never resort to such behaviour even if goaded. The door was then slammed on the offending features of Mrs. Evans and her bruised limb. She could be heard on the other side of it threatening violence to me and I immediately received the flying slipper treatment.

My mother was in the back kitchen poking at a pot on the stove.

"Is that you, Georgie?"

The name 'Georgie' at that early stage along life's bumpy pathway was anathema to me. The diminutive was not one of endearment, merely the method used to distinguish my name from that of my father, who was also named George. Thus, whenever the cry "GEORGIEEEEEEEE" went out I was not too sure whether the shit was about to hit the fan or my egg was cooked. I still shudder inwardly with embarrassment at the thought of the words chanted by young hoods and their future molls of "Georgie Porgie pudding and pie." I would launch stones, sometimes even half bricks, from a discreet distance whenever this offensive rhyme was chanted in my direction.

"Where have you been, and why are you dripping?"
"On the big field."
"What have you been doing?"
"Watching Spike 'avin a shag."

I was brought up to be truthful. I could have said, "Oh nothing, just playing." That morning I learned a lesson for survival. Never, ever, under any circumstances, tell the truth to anyone unless you are prepared to accept the full and furious consequences. In the matter of Spike the dog versus the truthfulness of Georgie, a severe blow was struck. Unlike my father, my mother had no reservations when it came to striking a child when she could apprehend it. Being a fairly nimble child was to my advantage, and all that usually happened in situations like this was the purposely misguided flight of a slipper whizzing past my head. However, on this occasion my mother's blast of fury exceeded my speed, and to this day my right ear still rings. I have since remained throughout my life extremely circumspect when asked by anybody what I have been doing.

"And don't do that again!" These words are indelibly cemented to my psyche. Never have they left me. Guilt springs eternal. They were many times spoken to me when I hadn't even done anything. I was often sent into a spin trying to remember what I was supposed to have done that I hadn't done which shouldn't be done again. If I ventured to ask what it was I was supposed to have done in the first place, the outcome was either the flying slipper treatment or a very stern admonishment not to be cheeky.

One matter which I certainly do remember being told not to do again on several occasions was walking backwards into lampposts. At one time I had sprouted two conspicuous lumps on the back of my head, which accounted for my father's acidic comment that I was probably knocking some bloody sense into myself so my mother shouldn't be too bloody concerned about it.

There were some things I never did, but for which I got told off along with the other rip stitches in the locality. I cannot ever remember being either cruel or hurtful to an animal, but I was accused of taking part in an unpleasant incident which horrified me in all my six years of earthly wisdom. It also caused me to enter into a passionate confrontation and subsequent bleeding nose with Arthur Evans, who accused me of such a monstrous act.

This happened when I was industriously reconstructing a bombed house from its blasted remnants. I was with Cyril Darch, a relative of the bookmaker (whose carpet my father had bought for him with his systematically unsuccessful up and down and doubles). Darch wasn't actually a friend, and he became an arch enemy some time later after he embedded a shard of slate in the temporal artery on the left side of my head, causing a great deal of blood and much consternation among the adults in the area who stemmed the flow by holding my head in a vice-like grip for about half an hour. It is not outside the realms of fantasy that the blood supply to my brain may well have been truncated during this operation and it was pointed out by my ever-knowledgeable father that this may well have been the reason why my brain was not all that it should have been when it came to matters educational.

On the opposite side of the bomb-site appeared the podgy figure of Yocker Spencer of the cleft palate, and sprightly Sonny Crummy of the solitary lung. They were in possession of a bicycle pump and were attempting to inflate a toad. They were Catholics, and although there were no serious vendettas between the younger children in the area, Protestants and Catholics kept themselves slightly aloof from one another. At that time I didn't know what a Catholic was, but I knew that Piggy the Priest was involved and whenever we Protestant children saw him, we ran away. There was a chant which used to be called out by older children to the priest which I could not understand, but which in essence was just one segment of a liturgical collection of abuse and bigotry directed towards Catholicism in general and the priesthood in particular:

'Av yer seen da priest

'Av yer seen 'is daughter

'Av yer seen her piss in da pot

An' call it holy water?

On King Billy's day, a motley gaggle of men and boys would march along Church Road past our house. A couple of drummers swaggered along, with some of the parade playing on tin whistles. They were led by a small boy playing the part of King Billy, wearing wellington boots and what looked like one of his mother's hats with feathers poking out from it. He was swinging a wooden sword (wrapped in silver paper) in time with the beat of the drums. Some of the men wore battered bowler hats and carried umbrellas. The more important-looking ones had long orange scarves draped around them. It puzzled me.

"Dad. Who is King Billy? Does he play for Liverpool?"

"No, son, not that King Billy. That King Billy has never been crowned. This one died a long time ago, and those fools need locking up."

"Why?"

"Because they hate Catholics. Your friend the nomark had better stay out of the way today, or he'll get pepper in his eyes."

No more needed to be spoken by my father. The gravitas of his voice when speaking with sincerity was always marked by the lack of the usage of word 'bloody', and his words rang authoritative and true to me when I was little. Indeed, they were fools and yes, they needed locking up. In fact I thought they all needed to go to Rainhill, the place I had been threatened with for not straightening my back and for kicking stones.

I learned from this short conversation that madness and prejudice are siblings and they are clothed in the cloak of extremes. Although it was ingrained at such an early age in my heart, I did not have the verbal skill to express such feelings, and still wonder at the magnificence of the talent of oratory.

*

Algernon, known locally as Algy the bookie's runner, was a personality admirably suited to his trade. He was inconspicuous in his surroundings and an affable local fixture. He was a tall thin pipe-cleaner of a man in the twilight of his years, but nimble enough to pedal his decomposing Hercules roadster at a canter whenever the local bizzie was seen approaching from a distance. He permanently wore his cycle clips ready for a quick getaway, a frayed cloth cap and a grey gabardine raincoat which flapped in the wind when he was forced to decamp at speed. He had a long pointed nose which seemed to have a perpetual dew-drop on the tip of it. He also whistled, and sometimes hummed, tunes from the shows. I was quite well acquainted with Algy, as was my father. On some days when I was training to play for Liverpool, kicking my treasured size-three football against the back doors of the Lion and Unicorn (I had found it washed up on the shore alongside what I thought was a deflated balloon with a knot in it), he would stand leaning on his bike giving me instructions on how to trap a ball and how not to kick it with the toe.

> "That's a toe-ender sonny, that's no good. Yew'll kick it over the bar if yew does that. Get yer noddle over the ball and use the top of yer foot. Don't lean back or yew will put it in the stands!"

His services were invaluable. I would deliver half-crown pieces wrapped in scraps of paper to him where our street corner met the back jigger, which was where he plied his illegal trade. He'd emit his tinny whistle through clenched teeth, furtively on the look-out for any signs of the constabulary. Only on one occasion do I remember going to collect some 'winnings' from Algy. He was rather circumspect in his attitude when I approached him.

> *"What's his nomdeeploom?"*
> *"What's his what?"*
> *"His NOM DEE PLOOM!"*
> *"What?"*
> *"Don't bother sonny, I know what is anyway. Here –*
> *don't lose it or spend any or I'll cut yer tail off. Tell*
> *him that his each way up and down and doubled yank*
> *worked for a change."*

I didn't tell my father anything of the sort for two reasons. First, I couldn't remember the detail of such a scrambled message and I am not sure that it has been correctly reported now, and second, the word 'yank' to my way of thinking was closely associated with another word I had heard in the company of Alfie Littlehales and repeated in the perilously close vicinity of the flying slipper, not knowing the meaning or connotations of the verb *to wank*. Nor did Alfie for that matter. At least if he did, he never imparted the information to me.

Algy arrived panting on the scene of the imminent explosion of a toad in the guise of the avenging angel, wobbling on his bike across a field of debris. He was out of breath and in a condition of some consternation, which was most unlike him.

> *"ME PUMP! GIVE ME ME PUMP, YEW THIEVING*
> *LITTLE BASTARDS!"*

This was certainly not the benign Algy of street corner whistling with whom I was acquainted. He had assumed the countenance of one who belonged in Rainhill, to which I was told I would be sent if I didn't stop behaving like a bloody lunatic, take my bloody hands out of my bloody pockets and straighten my bloody back. I can remember being threatened with being forced to wear a special brace to straighten it and was terrified by the thought, but was reprieved by the kind Dr Novak who told my parents that pneumonia was the source of my rounded shoulders and I would grow out of it. In retrospect he was doing his best to avoid my having to wear a brace, knowing full well that I would never change my posture – I am still round-shouldered and still walk with my hands in my pockets. Also, I still kick stones and empty cans whenever I see them – still daydreaming about the exploits of the great Billy Liddell whose spirit burns within me to this day.

Yocker Spencer, so named because of his speech impediment and the resultant spray of spittle which jetted out when he spoke, turned his tousled snot-daubed nine-year-old head to face Algy and spoke only two words.

"Huck ock."

Yocker didn't mince his words metaphorically, although he did literally. Fortunately for him, he had difficulty pronouncing the consonant 'f' which saved him a great deal of extra grief when remonstrating with officialdom.

"Give me me pump now, or I'll skin yew alive."

Algy dismounted his rusting cycle like some latter-day crusader ready to do battle. With one majestic swoop of his spider-like leg, his toecap scored a direct hit on the ragged rear end of Sonny Crummy, while at the same time his lumpy, blue-knuckled arthritic fingers regained a moment's dexterity, clamping them firmly on the jug-like protuberance of one of Yocker's ears which he twisted violently.

Only then did Algy realise what they were using the pump for. It fell to the ground, as did the toad which hobbled away under a nearby brick, unaware that it had very nearly been flaked alive had it not been for the fortuitous arrival of an old man on a bike.

"Yew nasty little sods. Yer not fit to breathe. I've got a
bloody good mind to pump YEW up!"

"Huck ock. Our Yonner'll get yew for dis yew old unt."

Another consonant which caused difficulty for Yocker was the letter 'c'. Yonner Spencer, his elder brother, would certainly have become involved in this scuffle had he not been serving a stretch in Walton jail, relative to his notoriety as a bad man. The ear was held in a vice-like grip as Algy bent down to administer some advice.

"Don't thieve me pump again or I'll 'av the police on to yew. And don't be crewel to dumb animals".

The confrontation was further enhanced by the arrival on the scene of the priest, a red-faced Irishman with a bulging blue-veined nose and a straining cassock.

"Now what in the name of our Lord is all dis about now? You'll be raising da dead with all dat racket so you will, so you will."

Yocker saw some light at the end of the tunnel. He knew the priest, and although they were not on first-name terms, the priest would be aware that Yocker was one of his strays.

"He's hittin' me farder, he's hittin' me. I 'aven't done nowt."

The priest took Yocker at his convoluted word and went off on a head-to-head with Algy, regardless of which Algy maintained a firm grip on the reddening ear of his prisoner.

"What's da matter with you Sir? Doesn't yew know what our Lord says about suffering little children? Let go of dis child immediately or I shall be forced to involve the constabulary, indeed I will, so I will."

"Oh yer will, will yer, you big fat bag of wind. Well,
I'll tell yer this, FATHER, the little bugger will suffer
more than a twisted ear if he steals me pump again,
and as for blowing up toads I'll bloody well blow 'im
up!"

Algy then became my hero. Not only was he a first-class football coach, but he'd saved the life of a toad and had faced up to the priest. I would have run away, but not Algy. He took a step towards the priest, extending his chin, unwittingly stretching the already oversized ear of Yocker, who let out a roar of anger, managed to release himself from the vice he had been held in and then disappeared into the unexplored territory of Chapel Street, an area strictly off limits to me, where – should I venture there – I would get bloody diphtheria and die.

"Don't you talk to me like dat. I am a man of God
don't yew know, don't yew know."

The priest was now inflating himself and his cassock strained even harder to keep his bulk within its confines.

"Oh, a man of GOD, are yew? Yews is a bloody big fat
clod-hopping busy body, that's what yews is."

Algy bent down, lifted the brick, gently retrieving the toad from its hiding place, and carried it to a clump of weeds in the corner of the bomb-site, where he deposited it. He returned to where he had left his bicycle, replaced the stolen pump on the frame, mounted the bike and wobbled away over the rubble and into the street. He turned his head when he reached the street, nodding momentarily in the direction of the now deflating priest. A tear was trickling down his wizened face.

"A man of God, ay, a man of God."

As he went on his way, he hummed – falteringly – the tune of *All Things Bright and Beautiful*.

What I learned that day was that goodness is not necessarily in the eye of the beholder.

*

Albert Faulkner had a dirty face and could draw horses' heads and cowboy hats. He taught me these skills, and also how to fashion a horse's head in plasticine. He wasn't of a very sunny disposition, Albert, and he appeared to get regularly picked on by our contemporaries resulting in adenoidal cataclysmic wailings when he was tied to a lamppost and they danced around him. Nonetheless, he was my friend and he was much more acceptable to my father, regardless of his dirty face and his foghorn-like blasts of anguish when captured by a hunting party on the warpath looking for a paleface to scalp, which was usually him. It was highly unlikely that he would lead me astray, unlike the nomark Littlehales. Besides, our mothers were acquainted and they lived just around the corner from us, about five yards from the lamppost which – when not being used as a totem pole or the upright for a rudimentary swing – I was always colliding with when walking backwards.

The Faulkners lived in an end-of-terrace at the top of Wesley Street quite conveniently next to a bomb-site. Like the bomb-site, it was devoid of furnishings. The table was covered in newspapers, and I distinctly remember drinking out of a jam jar while sitting drawing the heads of horses.

Mrs Faulkner was toothless, permanently wore a headscarf and overall, and always seemed to be purposefully shuffling somewhere in carpet slippers. She was a kindly lady, much worn down by strife. Her husband never spoke to anyone, probably not even to her, and walked with his head bent slightly sideways towards the ground as if he were looking for something. I believe he worked on the docks when there was work available, although there must have been many times when he trudged to the docks and found that his face didn't fit, because at that time getting work there was akin to attending a slave auction. The indignity of being herded like an animal into a shed alongside hundreds of other hopefuls desperate to be accepted for a day of back-breaking work on the whim of a gaffer who had his own agenda, was the probable reason why he didn't talk and walked with his head bent towards the ground. Mrs Faulkner scrubbed anything she could for other people in return for a few coppers.

Maisie Faulkner was betrothed to Ivor, an American GI stationed at Burtonwood airbase from where every mighty B17 Flying Fortress bomber that flew in World War II was assembled and maintained to return Germany's fire with remorseless intensity. I didn't come into contact with Ivor, nor did I see a great deal of Maisie, although I do recollect her as a willowy figure with long hair and with a bump in the front. I did benefit from her relationship with Ivor in the form of American candy and various other treats filtered down through Albert's muddy fingers. The muddy fingers were ever-present because of Albert's fixation with digging in the dirt with ice-lolly sticks in a quest to liberate ants from their underground prisons.

Not only was Albert a friend and liberator of incarcerated ants (except for the red ones, which bit him), but he was the custodian of a menagerie in his back yard. In an assortment of jars and buckets lived newts from the ponds in the public gardens at the bottom of South Road, frogs and toads reared from tadpoles, one of which was probably the cause of Algy's rant, and red-throated sticklebacks from the little stream which meandered alongside Sniggery Woods. An assortment of blood-suckers (pond life of indeterminate provenance) acquired from the canal was also incarcerated in an old enamel bowl and had to be approached with great caution. There was a grass snake that was once the pride of the zoo but had escaped and a pigeon with only one leg. Some of the frogs were my property. When they were tadpoles they had resided for a very short period in the decayed bath at 4 Church Road until an extremely serious discussion with my mother about my domestic responsibilities and that should the tadpoles still be in residence when my father returned home the plug would be pulled, they would be flushed away, and I would be severely dealt with by a man who never hit me.

Fortunately she was not at home the day the rat arrived in a cardboard box. It had been captured at the outlet pipe of a sewer disgorging effluent directly into the River Mersey which was an interesting play area for children when the tide was out. However, Martha was in residence and took the matter in hand with hardly a word said. The box containing the rat was stuffed into my mother's gas cooker and the supply was switched full on. A couple of minutes later the window was opened to disperse the fumes and negate the possibility of an explosion, and then the oven door was opened and out staggered the half-gassed rat. It was finally dispatched with an iron frying pan. My mother wasn't told of this incident, probably because a rat had been in her oven and her frying pan had been used as the ultimate weapon of destruction.

> *"Don't ever bring a rat in here again, or it will be your*
> *head that goes in the gas oven."*

I sincerely believed she was quite capable of gassing me. After all, she was in league with a butcher who would chop my fingers off and make them into sausages.

Sniggery Woods is no invention. It really exists, and was a haven for innocent adventure and the gathering of blackberries to be pooled by a group of fantasy warriors equipped with bamboo bows and arrows assembled from plundered canes from the gardens of the local landed gentry. The blackberries were taken back to Wesley Street for the construction of a pie built by Mrs Faulkner, along with the day's catch of sticklebacks in jam jars. The location of Sniggery Woods, which I thought was secret and only known to a select few, is two stops along the Liverpool-to-Southport line from Waterloo to Hall Road where the posh people lived. To me, people who lived in council houses were posh. It is situated about half a mile along a road from the station and down a narrow track which leads to a small bridge over a stream. This place was a haven serendipitous to a small child growing up on a fault line that separated affluence from poverty.

> *When all the world seemed full of fun*
> *Our childhood was a never-ending dream*
> *Of castles, kings, and wars we won*
> *On horses made of plasticine*

Our bamboo bows stretched taut with twine
Our arrows tipped with sticky roadside tar
We fought as soldiers of the line
And won imaginary war

The bomb-site bricks our forts became
And slates from blasted shattered roofs our floors
And stealing milk was thought fair game
From unsuspecting neighbours' doors

The berry's juice tattooed our chins
Its piercing thorns our untaught fingers ripped
The pillaged fruit bounced in our tins
As home against the setting sun we tripped
Its carmine shafts expunged our sins

The blood-red throat of stickleback
The golden silky skin of flashing newt
The shiny beetle, oil slick black
The admirals aboard their moot

The dog was more than just a friend
We understood the language of the bark
He often warned with shouts from round the bend
"Beware – the keeper of the park."

3

AWARENESS

Rheumatic fever came early in my childhood. It came earlier than my friendship with Alfie Littlehales and Albert Faulkner. I recollect little of it, apart from the pain, an inability to move, and my brother prodding me through the rails of my cot. I was nursed at home for about three months by my mother and the attention of Dr Novak, who called in regularly and even brought me sweets. I came to understand later that he was Polish and that he came from a world much more devastated than anything we in Britain could ever envisage, regardless of the near direct hit on Buckingham Palace (giving royalty the cause to brag that they were also suffering the same inconveniences as their loyal subjects in the East End of London), the blazing eruption of Bootle, and my father's scuffle on the roof of the Lion and Unicorn – next door to us – with an incendiary device which failed in its attempt to scorch to the ground an establishment frequented by the quasi-Apaches of the region, the warriors bloated with fire water and their women daubed in garish war paint. Some of them would urinate in our outside hallway after a night on the warpath. Others would even indulge in carnal activities in the jigger, the corner of which was Algy's patch during the day. The great sadness is that the Lion and Unicorn is still standing, whereas the German rubble machine managed to reduce to a heap of ashes the red-brick library only fifty yards away.

"Dad, I found a balloon in the jigger."

"It's not a balloon. Go and throw it down the lavatory now and wash your bloody hands."

*"It is a balloon – I've found one before on the shore
but I couldn't blow it up because there was a knot in
it."*

*"I will swing for this bloody child, Jean. IT IS NOT A
BLOODY BALLOON. THROW IT AWAY AND WASH
YOUR HANDS. Don't ever pick one of those bloody
things up again or you will get a disease and die."*

"Well what is it then?"

*"Never you mind what it is or what it bloody well
isn't, just do as you are told. And stay out of the back
entry."*

From this disjointed verbal exchange I learned that things
may not be what you think they are, regardless of whether they are
identical to what you think they are, added to which you can catch
a disease if you pick something up in the road and will probably die.
I still pick things up in the road but am very circumspect regarding
the manner in which I pick them up, and many years ago came to
distinguish between a contraceptive and a balloon.

My father sincerely regretted his hand in the fate of this house
of drunken dissolute blood-letting and mawkish off-key singing.
I enjoyed listening to it late at night. *Irene, Goodnight Irene* and
Cigarettes and Whisky and Wild, Wild Women wafted through our
bedroom window and are still contained in a rusting filing cabinet
in the cluttered vaults of my brain. For me, a fortunate aspect
concerning the pub next door was that I was never ever reproved
for the many happy and constructive hours I spent kicking a football
repetitively against the back doors of the Lion and Unicorn in the
optimistic and unfounded assumption that one day, as a result of my
constant and diligent practice, I would play inside-right for Liverpool
alongside the great Billy Liddell. An added attraction to my training
area would be the arrival of the draymen with their barrels of beer.
Instead of chasing me away, they would take a break and put me 'in
goal', kicking balls for me to practise my non-existent goalkeeping
skills and giving me tips on how to head the ball.

"I should have let the bloody place burn down for all the bloody good it's done."

When I was probably at the recovery stage from rheumatic fever, one day my mother told the broom to stop walking up the wall. Whether I was hallucinating or not I do not know, but what I do know is that she disappeared from my life for a short period. I believe, although I am not sure, that she had a nervous breakdown. I distinctly remember my father cleaning the grate and laying coal for the fire – something he had never done.

No doubt the combination of my illnesses – rheumatic fever, three broken arms before the age of seven and two bouts of pneumonia, to say nothing of severely abscessed ears, tonsils and adenoids removed, perennial bouts of impetigo, biddy infestation and boils on my neck as big as bloody gob-stoppers (according to my father) – was reason enough to mentally disturb my mother. Add to this the matter of my father's gambling on horses that ran like crabs and it is little wonder that she took too many Beecham's pills and tranquilisers, though to little effect.

And then there was my brother, over three years older than me and extremely smart. I could only draw cowboy hats, but he could draw speedboats and make paper aeroplanes. He also read books. Biggles was his favourite, which he read avidly. My weekly periodical was the *Dandy*. I thought he disliked me with an intensity which still stings, but in retrospect perhaps he had very good reason. I was a pain in the arse. I was always ill. My nasal passages were congealed with a substance not unlike candle wax; my ears discharged a smelly yellow gelatinous substance and I yowled a lot. To top it all, he was forcibly pressed into being my carer whenever we went outside to play cops and robbers in the street until I was about six years old. Because of my delicate medical condition he was sidelined in the parental care stakes and this no doubt caused him to be less than hospitable to a toddling whinger with various sticky substances running down the front of a shirt that once was his property. *"MICHAEEEEL! – where's our Georgie?"* was a cry which still subsists in his head to this day. He also took the blame for my proclivity for walking into lampposts backwards, getting covered in shite (some of which was the effluent disgorged from the business end of Spike), falling into ponds and getting stuck in the mud of the River Mersey when the tide was out.

As we grew, so did the mutual antipathy fuelled by my father, who was of the opinion that my brother should get his nose out of his bloody books and get out and emulate his younger brother who was in serious training to be Billy Liddell's right-hand man. His approval of my footballing aspirations and his unjustified denigration of my brother's literary aspirations gave me the edge in the skirmishes of our sibling rivalry. This was odd, because such a tirade of nonsense came from a man without any formal education at all, yet who not only owned Winston Churchill's *History of the English-Speaking Peoples* but had also read it, to say nothing of a whole set of *The Listener* collected throughout the period of World War II. He was a man who could quote Shakespeare, Longfellow and Tennyson, but he could never back a winner. He knew every bird and the markings of their eggs, he could catch a small fish in the canal with a bent pin on cotton baited with a piece of bread (which remarkable feat I evidenced), and he could take a Rolls Royce's innards to pieces and put them together again, which he did surreptitiously over the period of a week when he was given charge of one to service in the lock-up garage of the owner. The set of Churchill's *History* was stowed away among the treasures of my grandfather's store of souvenirs, until one day I noticed it was there no longer – Rosie's junk shop had gone upmarket, and I was sent by my mother with the shopping bag to load up with compressed coal-dust briquettes from a man at the railway sidings. Stowed away in the cupboard in our bedroom were my father's pin-striped trousers, a long white silk scarf and some very natty patent leather dancing shoes. They disappeared at about the same time as the books and no doubt took the same journey.

To know is not to be
There is no question
Knowledge is not power
But it can switch on a light

4

THE SCHOLAR

Zorro, Flash Gordon and Popeye-v-Socrates

*The ferry creaked against New Brighton's quay,
disgorging snotty kids with scabby legs, curse-wise
and cock-sure in their innocence. "We haven't paid
you, we haven't paid you, you fat old bastard, we
haven't paid you! "Scaling the pier to frighten New
Brighton; pint-sized Vikings marauding in the sun.
Scab-faced, pockmarked, rowdy dockers' offspring
with boils on their necks and lice in their heads.
Protégés of Empire's glorious sham and spawn of
war's magnificent broken vows. The truth behind the
lies which promised much, the lies behind the truth
that war was won.*

*Let them be. Don't anger them, let them be.
They've never been held, they've never been kissed.
They're off to New Brighton to see the rat as big as a
dog with teeth like a horse.*

*They're off to New Brighton to fight on the beach
and dig for some gold beneath the silt.*

*They'll beg for a tanner to buy an ice (a Pendleton's
Twicer is twice as nice). They'll bully the bourgeois
from Blundellsands and yocker their phlegm at the
maiden aunt. They'll frighten the donkey to make him
jump and stamp on the crabs because they're alive.*

*Then they'll go home to a plate of cold scouse. Back
to the city of Tate and Lyle's gold and into the realm
of the world of the slums. Running from the bizzie
down the jigger, laughing at the strength of weakness.*

Cursing creation and the love of Christ.

Yes, when I was about ten this was the world I knew a little of. I wasn't like them, but I shared guilt by association. I wore my brother's shoes, but never boots. My stitched-together trousers were washed, and the holes in the elbows of my brother's handed-down pullover were neatly darned.

There is a sort of wisdom that grows with age. It is more precious and much more painfully gained than the born-wise variety. It is self-realisation, not self-belief, and it always comes with hindsight. I had no idea I lived on a social fault-line which would be the catalyst for my pre-ordained journey through life. The words of Socrates, which I did not read until much, much later, rang true to me at the age of 10 through the heroic deeds of Flash Gordon – *it is not living that matters, but living rightly.* While Cherie Blair, who later lived around the corner from me on the other side of the fault-line, was doing her prep and the vitriolic Anne Robinson was learning all the withering skills of a pseudo upper-class poseur in Blundellsands – her mother was a market stall holder – I was learning philosophy from Popeye – *I am what I am, and that's all that I am,* morals from Superman – *I stand for truth and justice,* and ethics from Billy Liddell. I didn't learn much that made sense to me at all at school. *Ethics from Billy Liddell?* Yes, indeed. Zorro also lurked in the background, but cannot be categorised. I suppose I saw him as an example of triumph over adversity. To me, the exploits of Flash Gordon were no more fanciful than the adventures of Homer's Odysseus or Virgil's Aeneas. The ethics of Billy Liddell still ring true and in accord with those presumed to have been penned by Aristotle. Superman flew with the gods and made mock of mortal morality and feeble insouciance. The Three Stooges and the Marx Brothers were my introduction to the plays of Aristophanes. What is so advantageous to the unread is that in their world ancient Greek and Latin translations by Victorian academics are no requirement to getting the message; in fact the dusty archaisms associated with them cloud it. The magic of the silver screen turned the abstract declension of which I knew nothing and still know little, into the legitimacy of a language which did not require Greek and Latin translations to grasp the elemental force of literature. To enjoy rhyme and metre, and indeed to write it, one doesn't need to know anything of the mechanics of dactyls or assonance. They are-ever present in our language. The iambus is merely a heartbeat. Paul McCartney and Chuck Berry are living breathing evidence of this.

> *We come along on Saturday morning*
> *Greeting everybody with a smile*
>
> *Keep your sunny side up, up*
> *Hide the side that gets blue, do!*
> *If you've eleven sons in a row*
> *Football teams make money you know!*
> *Stand upon your legs*
> *Be like two fried eggs*
> *Keep your sunny side up!*

This, to the accompaniment of the flashing chromium rainbow-coloured gyrating organ, piloted by a nervous keyboard supremo dripping perspiration from his shiny balding pate, with heavy black horn-rimmed spectacles slipping down his nose and a black skewwhiff bow tie, drenched in a shower of apple cores, chewing gum, pellets of silver paper and screwed up sweet wrappers. The Odeon on Crosby Road was a place of learning far more attractive and informative than the dour official educational establishment of Wesley Street Methodist Primary School. I couldn't spell 'Odeon' then and had no idea that the word is of ancient Greek origin. To me the Odeon was the equivalent of the lecture hall I was never to know and life, real life, was portrayed and acted out by cartoon characters, movie star slapstick comics, and serious heroes and villains who won and lost respective trials and misfortunes. The goodie always won, the baddie always lost. Sylvester never made a meal of Tweetie Pie no matter how hard he tried.

"Well, here we are again children. It is nice to see so many happy, smiling faces."

"We want the picture, we want the picture, we want the picture, we want the picture."

"Now calm down, calm down. I've got one or two announcements to make."

"We want the picture, we want the picture, we want the picture, we want the picture."

"First of all, I have to tell you that you must not throw your chewing gum at the screen or stick it on the seats. The screen cost a lot of money and if it gets damaged we shall just have to close the cinema. Now we don't want that, do we children?"

"We want our money back, we want our money back, we want our money back!"

The organ again flashed and revolved, then struck up the bright cheery number *Happy Birthday to You*, and simultaneously a stampede of miniature wildebeest charged the stage all claiming it to be their birthday and therefore their right to a lollipop supplied by the unfortunate manager.

When the stampede was over and a semblance of relative calm was restored, with the organist revolving thankfully into musical infinity, time stood still for us all as the lights dimmed and the curtains opened. Sometimes the image of a lady in a flowing white gown holding a flaming torch aloft flickered onto the screen to delighted cheers from the audience. Sometimes it was a roaring lion, and sometimes a muscular man beating a large gong. It was time for Ollie to bash poor old Stan and for Trigger to thunder across the screen with Roy Rogers astride him chasing the outlaw in the black hat. The only goodie who wore a big black hat was Hopalong Cassidy. Bluto's guffaw was silenced once more by Popeye's bursting physique, transformed after the swift ingestion of a can of spinach. The winsome Olive Oyle was freed from Bluto's evil and shameless grasp by a blow struck from Popeye's anchor-emblazoned, muscle-bound forearm, his pipe spinning in his lips, sending the brutal Bluto disappearing skywards, spread-eagled and also spinning. *"Toot toot"* from the revolving pipe and *"yuk, yuk, yuk, yuk, yuk!"* from the chortling mouth of Popeye, and a heart-rending *"Oh Popeye!"* from the delightful and enchanted Olive Oyle.

After the film show was over, a posse of cowboys would go galloping down South Road to the anguish of tutting old matrons shopping and gossiping. Smacking themselves on their rumps and holding on tight to imaginary reins, the cowboys would be followed by several spitfires swinging to and fro in close formation along the road, with Zorro taking up the rear clad in a flowing navy blue raincoat fastened at the neck with a well-used rag around his face, wearing his cub cap back to front. Lassie ran round and round snapping at passers-by. Thomas Scott's bakery was on the way home and much fun would be had by telling the lady at the counter to mend her broken biscuits. And the song lingered on:

Stand upon your legs
Be like two fried eggs
Keep your sunny side up

Until the age of seven most of my time was taken up by pneumonia, yowling, drawing cowboy hats, breaking arms and walking backwards into lamp-posts. Eventually, when I did tentatively put my head through the door at Wesley Street Methodist Infants School minus tonsils and adenoids (the former having been mistakenly removed by an over-zealous surgeon at Bootle Hospital), deserted there by a very thankful mother, I was introduced to a diminutive trusty with a quiff and the shifty look of a tell-tale tit whose tongue should be bit. He was engaged by Miss Waynson, a lanky lady with the regulation corrugated hairstyle of the period and a set of teeth which would do credit to a pony, to show to me the complexities of drawing a house, a smiley face, and a Union Jack. Outside of his official duties he also instructed me in the skill required to pee higher than the top of a urinal and showed me a picture of a woman with no clothes on. He was intent on explaining to me the lack of penis, but my sage Alfie had already imparted this information to me a year or so earlier, and so I was able to explain that his theory relating to the absent penis (in that it was chopped off at birth) was mistaken. He didn't believe me. Later in the day he told Miss Waynson that I said she had a fanny. *Out of the mouths of babes and sucklings.* Of course, Miss Waynson reported the lie to my mother. On this occasion I was not subjected to the flying slipper, but my pocket-money was stopped and I was threatened with having my mouth washed out with soap and water if ever I were dirty again.

This was the reason why I missed two episodes of Flash Gordon, and the shenanigans of the Three Stooges. My blood boiled. In retaliation for his disingenuous and spiteful act, I tripped this child up in the playground. Unfortunately, as has predominantly been the sideways situation for me in life, I chose precisely the wrong moment to release my venom, because my act of petulant and violent revenge coincided with the entrance of Miss Waynson into the playground, briskly swinging her bell. I spent the rest of that day sitting on a stool in the corner facing the wall. It could have been worse. I wasn't required to wear the dunce's cap, although Jean Munro sometimes did, merely because she came from Seaforth and ponged, or so it seemed to me. However, Mrs Munro terminated this unusual and barbaric practice when she burst into the classroom interrupting a jolly rendition of *Jesus Wants Me for a Sunbeam.* She was a tall muscular lady with lank red hair, a long nose and a colourful vocabulary matched by a threatening demeanour. Miss Waynson was elbowed to one side with a glancing blow, and Jean Munro was taken by her scrawny arm and marched out of the dumbfounded class, picking up the dunce's cap on the way and carrying it out with her as a trophy. She never returned, and neither did the cap.

During the short period in which I was acquainted with Wesley Street Methodist Church Infants School, it seemed that when I was not singing hymns I was facing the wall. I was accused of much but was innocent of most. When a good deal of the lead was stripped from Wesley Street Methodist church roof, probably by Yonner home on parole assisted by his apprentice Yocker, both of whom had considerable experience in the liberation of scrap metal and the beneficial disposal of it, I was put in the frame again by the same child. Fortunately for me, this time his lie was unsustainable because I was only about three feet nine tall and even Miss Waynson could not be daft enough to imagine that I was capable of such a physically challenging feat.

Regardless of the Wesleyan approach to educating infants, I nevertheless learned the basic skills of reading. *Janet and John* were partly responsible for this, because I can still remember the wonder and awe I felt at the sight of these two scrubbed cherubs sitting in their limousine, their pristine images gazing out of a dog-eared book, with their daddy in a trilby sitting complacently at the steering wheel and mummy, wearing a scribbled-in moustache and spectacles, with a big hat on her head, carrying colourful boxes of niceties into the open car door from the adjacent shop with the proprietor at his entrance waving a cheery goodbye. Their images were unreal to me – unlike my hero Flash Gordon, spurting across the universe in a large flaming dustbin-shaped spaceship, Hermes-like, in tights and boots with a Robin Hood hat on his head sprouting a long feather, in his noble quest to rescue the Earth from the evil clutches of Ming the Merciless. Nevertheless, I became able to read expletives scrawled on walls as well as to scrawl them surreptitiously on walls myself in the company of the sage.

Another recollection I have of this period was the day that my midget tormentor, still obsessed with his misconception regarding the absence of external female genitalia, coerced the daughter of a fish and chip shop proprietor in South Road, to display to us her operation scar in the back yard of her father's premises. I considered it to be too high up her abdomen to have any connection with genital mutilation. She told us that it was an appendix operation scar. I was none the wiser at this disclosure, but the midget was insistent that the word *dick* was an abbreviation of the word *appenDICK,* therefore what she was displaying was her dick scar. The discussion came to an abrupt and unseemly termination when her father appeared at his back door brandishing a frying-pan and threatening to call the police.

My parents never learned about this incident because I was always sent for my chips to Mr Lloyd, who whistled while he fried. His shop was on the corner of Chapel Street, the street where I had been threatened with diphtheria if ever I set foot there. He was the competitor and a far superior chip fryer compared to the South Road chip shop, and he was also a kindly man who treated us to free chips if we brought in a bundle of old newspapers for him to wrap his goods in. Sadly his generosity was abused, because often these old newspapers were scavenged from dustbins on the way to his chip shop, and the four pennies provided for me to buy chips was secreted in a personal slush fund. It saddens me now to reflect that he must have thought that my parents read such scandalous rags as *Tit-Bits* and *Reveille.* It may be for this reason that many Mancunians' objectionable description of Liverpudlians being 'bin dippers' could possibly have a ring of truth about it.

When I was a little older, I had a humiliating experience regarding the matter of newspapers in exchange for chips in the form of an older brother of one of my soon to be new-found friends from the stable side of the fault-line. He was someone I should have despised, but at the time – in all innocence – I did not. He had an oily obsequious smile and an air of cunning malice. People from his side of the fault-line didn't exchange newspapers for food or eat jam butties. He confronted me in the road one day when I was on my way to the chip shop with a bundle of newspapers and taunted me viciously about the matter. I hotly denied my intent, but to no avail. This unpleasant confrontation affected me for many years, intensifying the foundations of an inferiority complex, the remains of which still exist. I had assumed that I was acceptable to his family, but a nagging suspicion that he poisoned this friendship still lingers.

From my first educational experience I learned never to tell anyone anything if it could be misconstrued by a third party, and never to eat chips out of newspaper, because I knew where some of that newspaper had come from. Also, regardless of what Miss

Waynson said, you do not need a space suit to travel in outer space as long as you stay inside the spaceship and it stays airtight. I still cannot draw a Union Jack. Cowboy hats are my forte.

*

I was soon out of the clutches of the Wesley Street Methodist academy of singing, praying and scaring little children shitless regarding what the devil does to naughty ones, and into the junior department of the big boys' school on Crosby Road. Although it was called the big boys' school, I was too short to be considered as such. The bigger big boys, aged over eleven, were stabled in adjoining premises which were fenced off from the smaller big boys for obvious reasons. However, the railings separating big from little were devoid of spikes and barbed wire, and so the occasional early-morning ambush of a hapless small big boy was all too easy. This was one reason why sometimes I arrived late to school and was castigated for it, although to be given a bad conduct mark was preferable to being hoisted over the railings and deposited in the crusher, an experience I managed to avoid until I became one of the big big boys, initially becoming involved in the stalking and catching little big boys at the behest of bigger big boys for them to perform their pants-pooing torture on. Because I purposely never managed to catch anyone, I was punished by experiencing the full and overwhelming agony of the crusher, a rudimentary device which was merely a narrow channel of tarmac between the railings and the big big boys' toilets, at the bottom of which was a brick wall. The unfortunate captured little big boy was deposited at the end of the channel and the big big boys lined up with their feet on the railings pushing backwards. It probably was not dissimilar to the late Middle Ages' custom for dealing with witches, although stones were piled upon them and not boys.

All the while, a very big big boy – the architect of the procedure – would be at the entrance to the crusher on the lookout for Gotch, a teacher with extremely baggy trousers and a Hitleresque hairstyle, who was renowned for his stealth and ingenuity when creeping upon a malefactor, grabbing him by the neck, shouting *"GOTCHA"* and frog-marching him off to the headmaster for six of the best. Toilet malingerers were easily caught by Gotch, who took pride in waiting until he could see the spirals of smoke appearing over the top of the urinal wall and then pouncing like a lion after gazelles. I was terrified of him even before I was elevated to the big big boys section of school society. I once saw him watching at me over the dividing railings with a beady-eyed frown when I was standing on top of a heap of recently delivered coke, beating my chest and calling out to no-one that I was king of the castle.

The Rubicon was still to be crossed; I was only eight years old at the time so still had a couple of years before Gotch would be in a position to sink his talons into my neck. In the meantime I had the less formidable, but the more deviously sadistic, Miss Nelson to worry about, coupled with even more singing of unintelligible jingles.

Miss Nelson was a dour spinster of indeterminate age. She was stern, poker-backed, grey in clothing, complexion and hair – a monochrome person – and she didn't like children. If anyone coughed they were in deep trouble and were sent to sit outside the hall. The regular coughers were instructed to sit on their hands at the front of the hall and told that if they felt a cough coming on, they must swallow it. There were times when I went purple trying to swallow a cough and on one occasion I filled my trousers. Because the resultant smell seeped into all corners of the hall, it was impossible to tell where it was coming from, and to disguise my guilt in this matter I joined in the general expressions of revulsion.

"Which one of you has made that disgusting smell?"

A major coughing fit ensued among the budding reluctant choristers interspersed with cries of protestation resounding through the hall.

"Sometimes you children behave like animals. You
should all be kept in a zoo."

She slammed down the lid of the piano, gathered together her music and strutted out of the hall with a handkerchief to her face.

46

Moments later, a grinning caretaker tottered in, opened all the windows and told us we could go home.

That afternoon I dawdled through the back streets in the uncertain hope that the smell would abate before I reached home. It didn't, because when I arrived on South Road opposite the railway station, Jack, the diminutive bent-backed First World War veteran paper-seller who wore his campaign medal on his threadbare overcoat, told me so when I asked if he could smell me. He must have felt sorry for me, because he gave me a penny. He was charged by my mother with the onerous task of scuttling across the road with me every day, a dangerous feat for him to perform in view of the fact that his face was bent towards the ground. Because of his bent back he took more time and risks than me, had I crossed the road alone. And so I accepted that I was in the shit both literally and metaphorically and approached our home with a mixture of fear and apprehension. My anxiety was unfounded. A kettle was boiled and I was debagged, washed down and given a jam butty. My trousers and underpants were taken away for washing and I was kitted out in a voluminous pair of my brother's underpants. The matter was never spoken of, even to my father.

Miss Nelson's piano-playing skills were undoubtedly concert-hall standard, although her renditions of *Lavender's Blue Dilly Dilly*, *Old Father Thames Keeps Rolling Along* and *Caw, Caw, the Carrion Crow* became lost in the myriad of trills and musical affectations which so overpowered the melodies that they became drowned in an ocean of superfluous crotchets, quavers and demi-semi-quavers, thus causing her even more angst to add to the coughing outbreak encounters and the phantom pants filler. When she was really on form her body would follow her fibrillating fingers all the way along the keyboard to such a degree that falling off her stool became a distinct possibility. A further difficulty which plagued the singers was in the comprehension and transcription of the lyrics to these mellifluous refrains, which were always scribbled at speed on the blackboard by Miss Nelson in *real writing*, and then erased before anyone could employ their new-found writing expertise successfully.

And that's about all I can remember of the little big boy's school. What I learned for the future is that being late can be advantageous to one's health regardless of the disadvantage of censure, that to embellish music is to destroy melody, and that sometimes if you believe you are guilty of what some think is an offence, you may not be, and you might not be punished. Indeed, you may well be rewarded for your fortitude.

5

THE PARADOX

My father cursed constantly, unless he was being very, very serious and then articulation poured out of him with scant use for expletives. Although the word 'bloody' was of a minor significance in offensive terminology, it was the source of much embarrassment to me when friends visited. We lived, until Martha absconded with her alleged treasure, in primitive surroundings close to – but never part of – the small pocket of poverty on the one side and the relative material comfort on the other. Why was this? At the time I didn't know and really didn't care. Happiness to me was contained in a tin of condensed milk. Just off Church Road ran a leafy suburban lane occupied by people with brass signs outside their doors – late Victorian and Edwardian town-houses surrounded by spacious and well-tended walled gardens whose apple and pear trees were ideal plunder for the likes of Alfie Littlehales with me in tow.

One day, alone in a quest to liberate some apples from the garden of one of these houses, I was confronted by a tall graceful old lady with half-moon spectacles, her silver hair arranged in a bun. I had seen her quite often leaving her house with her shopping basket and striding purposefully along the road. Her house had a brass plate on the door. Her name was Miss Shaw, and she had the letters BSc engraved alongside her name.

"Come here young man, I'd like a word with you."

I didn't run away, but stood my ground transfixed on her lawn. She didn't seem in the least surprised to see me standing frozen under her apple tree. It wasn't the first time I had climbed over her wall, and she must have observed my juvenile criminal activity from her window. Over a long washing line was thrown a large carpet. She had a cane carpet beater in her hand and was peering at me in a stern fashion over her spectacles. I assumed the carpet beater in her hand was going to be transformed into a trouser beater, but my instinct for self-preservation abandoned me and I remained rooted to the spot.

"Do you think you could beat the dust out of this carpet for me? If you can, then I will give you sixpence."

I couldn't believe my luck. Not only did she give me sixpence for my feeble attempt to beat her carpet, but a glass of home-made lemonade and a biscuit. This fortuitous encounter became a regular source of private income and biscuits. Miss Shaw became a trusted confidante who would sometimes talk to me of her past travels, the places she had been on the other side of the world, and how the world shows many kindnesses regardless of the horrors of war. I didn't really understand what she meant then, but now I do, having in later life been entertained at Madam Hoo Ha's canteen with palm wine, ceremonial kola nuts and bats' head soup in a mud hut village deep in sub-tropical African bush by good, caring and much-maligned people. They once tried to make Biafra independent from the nonsense of a country cobbled together and composed of many disparate African nations and cultures, devised by a white man and named Nigeria by his fanatically colonialist wife. Three million of them perished whilst the British government under Harold Wilson, of all people, blockaded humanitarian aid, secretly supplied enormous quantities of arms and ammunition to the corrupt and inept federal government and watched as food rotted on the quayside. John Lennon, to his everlasting credit, returned his OBE in disgust and said why. These people lost not just limbs but whole families, yet even now still manage to retain their sanity.

What I did learn from Miss Shaw was that some of those who are privileged by fate to live on the comfortable side of the fault-line are not without genuine concern for those who, because of the throw of the dice, occupy less privileged territory. Unfortunately, there are not enough of them.

The barrier between the sedate dwellings of Miss Shaw and her neighbours and the adjacent small area of dismal little cobbled streets was the Winter Gardens picture house – Gomorrah without the sodomy. This place smelled bad, and fleas were definitely part of the programme. The odd rat had also allegedly been seen on the premises, cruising the aisles. We lived just fifty yards from this pit of lurid cinematography which would show films that would now be rated as fairly mild titillation, but to Alfie Littlehales were the bedrock of his source of information regarding the nature of all things carnal. Of course, a spindly spotty child suffering from impetigo would never have been able to con his way through the door, regardless of the relaxed attitude of the management. So industry and cunning overcame the obstacle of the doorman in the form of a nail, which he used to bore a tiny hole through the rear exit doors, small enough to take in half the screen but not large enough to be noticed by anyone cleaning the place, unlikely though this was. Sound was a problem, but a minor one. More important for Alfie were the moving visual images of ladies in swimsuits.

So why was I in this indeterminate area of no-man's land, sandwiched between feast and famine? We weren't poor, but we didn't have money. My father, to his ignominy, would come home on some Friday evenings and stand in a corner of the room with his back to us, counting out from his wages what he thought would be sufficient for our needs the following week and handing it to his benign and nerve-wracked wife. When this did not happen it was probably because he had lost most of his wages on a horse before coming home. What was left was fodder for the bookmaker, whose carpet had been bought with my father's wages, or so he said, via the horses which, like me, came out of the stalls sideways. We didn't own a carpet until much later on. Until the day she died, my mother never owned a washing machine or a fridge. Milk was kept cool in a bucket of water and a vacuum cleaner was something which other people had and was hardly a necessity anyway because of the lack of a carpet. Hot water only ran on some Sundays. Much to my lasting shame, I took on board my father's misogynistic paternal attitude towards domestic requirements, unaware of the basic needs of a family until later life and experience showed me the error of my ways, but by that time it was too late to show normal parenting skills regarding what a family needs and what a family wants. But he knew things, and he never hit me.

One thing he did know was that under no circumstances were we going to leave the home we had, crumbling though it might be. The way he saw it – although I had no idea at the time – was that the fault-line, for all its inconveniences and social uncertainty, for me was a far, far better place to be than living on a faceless estate even if the house there had hot water, three bedrooms, an upstairs lavatory, a garden and electric sockets. For this reason, when we were offered a place near the top of the post-war re-housing waiting list, he refused without telling my mother, opting to stay put. At least we were close to the shore and the relative urban decorum existing in Waterloo generally. Besides, he had several retainers in the area maintaining motor vehicles.

One of these retainers was for a lady who was in effect one of the reasons why my childhood was as happy as it seemed to me. Irene Johnson was the proprietor of G W Johnson, Builders' Merchants, and she was our landlady. The flat above her offices in which we were ensconced was her contribution to the war effort. As my parents had been 'bombed out' of their home in Bootle, Miss Johnson had come to the rescue. The place was crumbling, there was no doubt about that, but her generosity was such that the rent she charged was a pittance.

She was an enormous lady who spilled out over her bicycle when she laboriously plodded along Church Road as stately as a galleon in her olive-green overcoat and basin hat with a flower in it, from her home on the verge of Marine Crescent facing the Mersey, the most delightful aspect of Waterloo which was once home to Victorian sea captains and shipping magnates of Liverpool, the most famous of whom was Thomas Henry Ismay, founder of the White Star Line and owner of the Titanic.

Miss Johnson looked for the entire world like a good friend of the 1950s British film comedy actress Margaret Rutherford, and she had a certain manner in her speech and facial affectations which affirmed this. She lived in comfortable and genteel surroundings with Emily, a lady I believe was her American cousin, who was of similar although slightly less unwieldy construction and who once tried to dose me with a tablespoon of syrup of figs because she believed I was 'looking off colour'. In their garden was a large oak tree which I climbed up and refused to come down until the syrup of figs was replaced in the kitchen cupboard. They both ate vast amounts of chocolate, some of which came my way whenever I paid a visit.

They were both Christian Scientists, and were adamant that the body could heal itself without the aid of medicine men. Miss Johnson once confronted the medical profession head on, when her bicycle wobbled a little too far, hit the kerb, and all twenty stone of her crashed to the ground outside the offices of the *Crosby Herald*. Both to her dismay and anger a passing young journalist witnessed the incident and a report was duly filed with his editor. Despite a broken ankle and severe bruising, not only did she refuse medical assistance but got back on her bike and wobbled off home. She was in her eighties at the time. The broken bone was never set and the twisted limb became a deformity which she refused to acknowledge. I believe she went on to live well into her nineties.

"Now Georgie Porter, what have you been up to? I saw you climbing a wall yesterday. You weren't stealing apples were you? I have already told you we have an apple tree and you can collect the windfalls whenever you want."

"I wasn't, Auntie Reenee."

"Well then, what were you doing on that wall?"

"Practising climbing, Auntie Reenee."

"You're not telling me a fib are you, Georgie Porter? You know I have told you before that Jesus won't be happy if you are fibbing."

"No Auntie Reenee. I was practising climbing."

"Well here's sixpence, go and buy an ice cream and be a good boy."

Whenever she saw me, there was always a possibility that she would give me sixpence, so I made it my business to make myself available every time I caught sight of her lumbering along Church Road. She was aware that Algy, the mendacious bookie's runner, plied his dodgy enterprise from the corner of her business premises opposite the Lion and Unicorn, probably because he had a loyal and regular patron in the form of my father, and I would sometimes see him beating a hasty retreat on his bicycle with his coat tails flapping in the wind, pursued by a very large elderly spinster also on two wheels, but unable to catch him.

On Christmas Eve I would wait excitedly for a surprise at the bottom of our dank stairs, and was never disappointed. After the shop closed, two small brown envelopes would be dropped through the letterbox, clattering to the floor, one addressed in fine copperplate handwriting to my brother, and one to me. They contained two half-crowns for each of us. No message or card. Just the half-crowns, but I knew who had posted them, for I would see her substantial frame in the porch through the frosted-glass front-door window as she bent to post her glad tidings to two little boys.

Her generosity didn't end there. Not only did my father service her cousin Emily's car on Miss Johnson's behalf, but sometimes it would be lent to him to take us all out for a day at weekends. This is where we crossed the fault-line into the world of affluence and became posh for a day, driving along the Dock Road through wastelands of bombed-out buildings, some with people still – after four years – enduring life among the debris. Pinched women in headscarves and curlers hobbled through the muddle, some dragging bespattered little bundles of children along with them to and from I knew not where. Groups of ragged men with their necks hidden by mufflers and caps would stand around open fires fuelled by splintered wood. These were the people who never even got a foothold on the fault-line, the destiny for most of them being even more uncertain than mine. But for the grace of Irene Johnson and her crumbling remnants of Mr G W Johnson's Victorian merchant's residence there walked I, though little I knew it at the time.

On we would travel through the spicy aromas of cargoes delivered from around the world and into the jaws of the smoke-blackened magnificent city, along past St George's Hall, Liverpool's strident reply to Athena's Parthenon, and the mighty Royal Liver Building which was the first skyscraper in England, with its pair of mythical Liver Birds attached to the tops of its twin towers. My father said that they flapped their wings at one o'clock in the morning to try to escape but that they would never be able to because he had bolted them down securely so that they couldn't fly to Germany. I believed him. Later in life I discovered that his tale *("that's one with a lid on it!")* was pertinent to the construction of these world-renowned beasts. It is a strange but true irony that the man who created the eighteen-foot tall copper creatures, half gull and half cormorant, was a German. Carl Bernard Bartels, who came to Liverpool in 1887 at the age of twenty-one, took up British nationality, but nonetheless was sent to a prisoner-of-war camp during World War I and then was repatriated to Germany at the end of the war, having to leave his family behind. Not many people in Liverpool were aware that the Liverpool blitzkrieg was being watched over by a pair of mythical birds designed by a German.

Sometimes on the way in to Liverpool we would catch a close-up glimpse of the Mammoth – then the largest floating crane in the world. I had often seen her from the shore a couple of miles away because her home was the Gladstone Dock and occasionally she would venture out into the Mersey. From a distance she looked enormous and when we got close, her two-hundred-foot high jib made me feel like an ant. My father, the fount of all knowledge except for the winning capability of race-horses, said she could lift two hundred tons in one lift and he equated this to about one hundred and fifty cars. He told me that she was sunk in an air raid during the war, but Winston Churchill said that even though she was so enormous she had to be refloated, because we couldn't win the war without her. She was, and we did.

And then we would drive into the exciting undersea vault of the Mersey Tunnel, which at the time was the longest underwater tunnel in the world. This, for me, was the most exciting and yet unpleasant part of the day out. Travelling underneath the River Mersey for two miles in a motor car twisting and turning through a giant shiny tube and popping out at the other side to look back over the river and see the Liver Birds standing with their wings outspread and the massive sandstone soaring gothic bell tower of the Anglican cathedral, the largest bell tower in the world, gave a graphic indication of just how far we had travelled underwater. Halfway through the tunnel I would be violently sick. I dreaded this regular occurrence on our outings and a paper bag was always at the ready to deal with the regurgitated aniseed balls which were one of the only sweets not on ration.

> *"I can't bloody stop here. I'll swear he does it on purpose. If he makes a bloody mess on the seat I'll skin him."*
>
> *"It's coming out red George, he's coughing up blood."*
>
> *"It's not bloody blood, it's the bloody rubbish he's been bloody eating."*

And of course, it was. As well as knowing everything, he was perceptive.

An hour or so later, after a further aniseed ball crisis against the walls of Cammel Lairds shipyard, we were in North Wales and heading for the Horseshoe Pass, a world away from the debris of Scotland Road; a biblical vista breathtakingly awesome to the eyes of one so small, with its magnificent green crescent sweeping steeply downwards from the grey twisting ribbon of the road, dotted in the far distance with the white specks of sheep on patchworks of different shades of green. Then I would be told things from the man who knew everything but who couldn't back a winner. Through a haze of cigarette smoke he would show me the quarry (where all our depleted roof slates came from) gouged out of the pass, how the men worked and lived at the quarry, talk of the purity and sweetness of our Liverpool water courtesy of Wales' Lake Vyrnwy, point out Snowdon's peak, the Seven Sisters hills, Denbigh Castle which dated back seven hundred years, and more.

On other days we would travel north to the Lake District, but always to my regret by-passing Blackpool on the way. *"No. You are not going to Blackpool. It's a bloody den of vice."*

The Lakes then had not been completely besmirched by the motor car or Wallace Arnold. I would be taken to Grasmere, visit

Wordsworth's grave and Anne Hathaway's cottage, eat Kendal mint cake and be sick again. My father would show us the host of golden daffodils, recite the relevant snatch of Wordsworth, and drive right over the giddying heights of the grey-bouldered Honister Pass, the car struggling all the way up and whining in second gear all the way back down, with my mother grimacing on the tortuous winding descent. He would point to a soaring brown buzzard, a skylark, or a speckled song thrush and stop to sample pure silver Lakeland river water.

Five or six years later I would travel there alone at weekends on the bus to Ambleside from Crosby bus station and lose myself high up in the magnificent wilds of Hellvellyn and sleep in the open among the rocks by the tarn just below the summit, careless and safe in a world which no longer exists for children, occasionally woken amid the iridescent blaze of the stars by an inquisitive sheep and wonder if a man would ever travel among those stars like Flash Gordon. I didn't have a tent, but it never seemed to bother me. I wrapped myself in a blanket. In the morning I would knock on a farmer's door to buy some milk and eggs and would occasionally be given them free of charge by his wife with a warning to take care on the fells. I would build a little fire from twigs, boil my eggs and then heat up some beans. Due to my father's inexhaustible supply of information about everything, I learned to distinguish between ash, elm, birch, beech and alder. Ash was the best to burn and birch was a close second. Asleep one evening on a bench on the little green in Grasmere I was woken by a policeman concerned for my wellbeing, not to harangue me, but again to warn me to take care and to be a good boy. I did, and I was. Those days of singular carefree delight are gone and shall never return. To have known those days is a blessing, and it still warms the blood in my silted-up arteries whenever I think of them, despite the many years of good and not-so-good experiences which have intervened.

Sometimes when Miss Johnson's cousin Emily's car was not available, which was more often than not, we would walk to Seaforth Sands. There must have been sand there at one time, but when we used to walk the couple of miles there from Waterloo it was the beginning of the docks and the first station along a railway of great repute which was affectionately known as the dockers' umbrella; the Liverpool Overhead Railway. To travel on this line was a unique and privileged experience the like of which will never be known again, for it was an iron and steel testimonial to the ingenuity and industry of a generation of engineers. It was built by the people for the people and engendered a warmth of feeling which sometimes stems from man to machine and is inexplicably reciprocated by the structures themselves. Like a huge tree, it grew out of the road and spread itself over the docks, providing shelter from the elements for thousands of dockers beneath its rumbling overhead tracks, and its innovative passenger carriages that housed the electric motors beneath the floor which became the forerunners of electric railways the world over; in fact it was the world's first overhead urban electric railway, and became the revolutionary model which is still employed today on the London underground.

For over six miles we would traverse the docks which harboured great liners and pass by Princes Landing Stage at the Pier Head, another great wonder – the largest floating landing stage in the world when it was built. Because it floated, passengers could embark and disembark regardless of the tides. I have a vivid memory of seeing close up the sad and haunting sight of one of these great liners, the *Empress of Canada*, wallowing on its massive crumpled side with its enormous funnels smashed on the wall of Gladstone Dock. There had been a fire and she had sunk. My father explained these things to me without cursing, enthusiastically divulging his knowledge to me while I overdosed on aniseed balls which only made me sick when travelling in a car or on a bus – never in a train. Certain information he kept to himself; shielding his knowledge of the internal combustion engine and its workings was his own self-centred realm, something of which we were not to question and which to me is still clothed in mystery.

And therein rests the paradox. This man who couldn't back a winner knew more than any man, but I was stuck on the fault-line – seeing and learning more than children of a settled background, many of whom I later became friends with, but still looking at them from afar, unable to do my twelve times table. And so it has remained, regardless of my relative success in life – well book-read, travelled and self-educated with a good degree – but nonetheless still with a feeling of inadequacy towards them. I was deemed a failure at the age of ten by the State because Flash Gordon was my Hermes and it was Superman who flew with the gods. An essay describing the endeavours and the moral values of these two giants of my childhood literary admiration would never have been contemplated as a fit subject for an eleven-plus examination. Also, how are babies made? It would not only have been extremely inappropriate, but outrageous to enquire whether a child of ten should even contemplate discussing such things, especially in the colourful but clearly descriptive vernacular used by Alfie Littlehales. Odysseus would have been just the ticket had I heard of him. If I had taken more interest in the fictional life and times of Biggles, rather than the just-as-daft exploits of Korky the Cat or Jack's Magic Patch, perhaps I would have followed in my brother's be-capped and rugby-booted scholastic footsteps. But what use would football have been to me when they all played rugby?

The eleven-plus examination, as it was constructed in the early 1950s, has now been discredited by most right-thinking people, but its legacy was a blemished – though thankfully a disappearing – slice of society. I have read that only twenty percent of my generation actually went to a grammar school, and the vast majority were boys who came from the more prosperous sections of society. We who didn't, on the other hand, were the children of a war-ravaged country who, during our formative years, were encouraged to believe that we were intellectually incompetent, though in fact it was more about our social position, and our inability to understand concepts and mores which were socially beyond our grasp. Most of us were never even given the opportunity to acquire any formal qualifications. I only began to think of myself as uneducable when I realised that I would never be able to learn French and that Latin was not for me. I had seen a Bunsen burner, but never been allowed within arm's length of one. I had played with some iron filings and a magnet, but for what reason I did not know. Geometry was never mentioned, although my brother had a set of compasses and some sort of triangle with markings on it. Algebra is to this day a mystery to me, not because I would have been unable to learn, but because my career path would not involve acquiring such knowledge, and so it was.

If children completed what education was offered by the age of fifteen, they were given a school leaving certificate. In my case I didn't even get that. I was allowed, not to say encouraged, to leave school at fourteen to join the Army. We could never aspire to be doctors, lawyers, army officers, teachers or scientists, although a small few did; most of them through dogged determination not to be labelled a failure at such an early stage in life. Ask John Prescott, and he will tell of the struggle he had to achieve his potential, purely because he failed his eleven-plus. From merchant seaman to deputy prime minister, to a peerage. The back-handed compliment *"they failed their eleven-plus, but they managed to get on anyway"* is all the more galling for those who didn't 'get on' and never realised that they were capable of so much more than they had been told they were worth.

6

NEW PERSPECTIVES

I began to realise I could never eradicate my past: that the circumstances of my birth would dictate my position in the world, just as it did for someone from a more established section of society. It was nothing to do with brain-power. In the words of Popeye – *I am what I am*. At the age of eleven I became aware that I bestrode a fault-line – my world contained things that were unknown and inconceivable to many of my new-found friends at Sunday school, in the church choir, or in the boy scouts, who came from more stable backgrounds. I began to cast off my old friends who lived on the fringes of our humble society and – sad to say, but it's the truth – I became embarrassed to be seen in their company. I now had newer, less unkempt children to associate with.

Albert was refused entry to the church choir when I tried to enlist him, not because he could not pitch his voice in tune with a note from the piano, but because he still had a dirty face. Alfie, the nomark, disappeared off my radar because he wore boots and would have no truck with Protestantism wihout really knowing what it was and so bolstering the ignorance of prejudice, and Yocker probably followed in his elder brother's footsteps. In short, I became a walking contradiction, because my societal horizons were broadening but my ingrained conceptions of where I fitted in the world were embedded in my mind, and have remained so ever since. Sunday school, the choir, and the boy scouts were initiated into my rather hectic schedule of football practice, limb breakages and keeping my sunny side up by my father, who – although a stranger to all things outwardly religious – I had sometimes seen kneeling at the side of his bed saying his prayers in his shirt-tails late at night, assuming I was asleep. Perhaps, I thought, he was praying for the elusive winner.

Sunday school didn't last too long. I was hit over the head with a very heavy Bible by a religious maniac called McFie, because I questioned that a man was able to walk on water. Also there was the matter of the broken window in the church hall, the outcome of a misdirected tennis ball with a toe-ender. McFie was mad enough to call round to 4 Church Road and confront the man who knew everything and prayed late at night in his shirt-tails. My lack of faith, coupled with a propensity for vandalising church property, was his opening denunciation of me, followed by his professed concern for my safety in respect of my spirited pastime of wall-climbing. My father received McFie seated by the fire in his decaying creaking armchair dotted with darned cigarette burns, amid clouds of smoke and rivulets of ash running like a volcanic emission down the front of his jacket. The *Sporting Life* lay sprawled on the floor. Grimaldi, the black witch's cat, whose main purposes in life seemed to be digesting left-overs and defecating in various corners of the house regardless of an ever-open window to allow him to come and go as he pleased, was curled on my father's knee in hissing mode. McFie, who must have thought he had entered a court of Beelzebub, turned pink with discomfiture.

> *"Are you the one that hit my son on the head with a bloody big bible?"*
>
> *"Yes – he doubted the word of God, and I am sure you wouldn't approve of that."*
>
> *"I don't approve of anyone hitting my boy; I don't even do it myself. His mother does sometimes if she can catch him."*
>
> *"That's probably why he is so wayward."*
>
> *"Wayward? What I call bloody wayward is hitting a child over the head with a bloody big bible. Do you know what I call that? I call that bloody sacrilege, that's what I call it. It would do you some good to read it rather than beat bloody children with it. I know it says something about suffering the little children. And don't you give me any of that spare the rod and spoil the child nonsense either."*

62

"I don't think I've ever seen you at church, Mr Porter."

*"No you haven't, and you're not bloody likely to either,
although I'll lay you a fiver that I know more about
the bloody bible than you ever will – I had it rammed
down my throat, not slammed over my head. Now
bugger off."*

I cringed. McFie departed chastened. Then the man who didn't
hit children turned to me.

*"And you, you daft little sod, behave yourself or it will
be more than a bible you'll get over your head – it'll
be my belt across your backside."*

I was thenceforward relieved of my obligation to attend Sunday
school, and it was just as well because there were several other
matters which may have come to the fore. Had McFie been made
aware of my alleged involvement in the incident regarding a boy's
cub cap and the bear pit at Chester Zoo on a Sunday school outing,
even more flak would have flown.

*

Martha had died when I was nine. She and her alleged substantial
trove of treasure, including the piano which purportedly creaked
with concealed fivers, was gone. One day nearing the end of her life,
the piano had been spirited away in a furniture van by my mother's
sister, a lady I barely knew, but who was physically on a par with
Mrs Evans. Although the way she dressed clearly placed on her
affluent side of the fault line, she was still more than capable of
frightening the horses. Bessie Braddock, that remarkable Liverpool
MP of great fortitude and charisma, who once called Churchill a
drunk to his face and forcefully carried a visiting high-ranking Tory
politician from a house especially prepared cosmetically for his visit
into a neighbouring slum, could well have been her doppelganger.
Although they looked alike, Bessie Braddock's face did not match
the rigid set of this woman's attempt at a smile, nor did it betray

63

the distinct aura of haughtiness which surrounds a certain type of northern matron depicted so admirably by the late Les Dawson. She was my aunt, and I can remember only meeting her on two occasions, but she may well have been a contributory factor in my mother's mental malaise. My grandmother died in a Liverpool hospital which had, in earlier days, been the workhouse from whence she came – or so she believed – and her last hours must have been a dreadful experience for that reason. None of the contents of the groaning piano found their way back to 4 Church Road, nor were they spoken of again.

Earlier that year my brother had become one of the few who had actually passed the entrance exam to the grammar school ("*by the skin of his teeth*" grudgingly acknowledged by my father) where he became involved in singing bizarre songs. *Nymphs and Shepherds Come Away*, *The Raggle Taggle Gypsies Oh* and something about jolly boating weather were cases in point. What was a nymph and where were they all coming away from? I was very excited for him, although I was unaware of what this fuss about a grammar school meant. I did, however, link this achievement to his fixation with Biggles, which he read avidly to the detriment of his footballing skills and the despair of our father. With his elevation to the higher echelons of learning came a smart uniform, a cap, a satchel, and a very natty sports shirt. Also he was given a present of a Newmark watch which, for a reason that baffled me, he refused with disdain, and it lay in the drawer of the sideboard in its box until the day I cleared the remnants of my mother's meagre belongings many years later, after she had died. I was soon to learn that on one side of the fault-line Newmark watches were prized possessions, whereas to the children on the other side, where the posh people who subsisted in council houses lived, a Newmark watch was not acceptable.

> "*Where we're going to get the bloody money from for a uniform, I don't bloody know. And rugby boots! He couldn't hit a bloody barn door from ten bloody yards.*"

As usual the grumbling was bluster. A uniform did appear, including a cap and a pair of rugby boots. Out of malice I sometimes hid his cap just when he was about to leave for school. The boots were handed down to me a year later in pristine condition, but a size and a half too big. Nonetheless I was very proud of them and wore them with the toes stuffed with newspaper, disregarding the contemptuous chants of 'Charlie Chaplin' from my brother and his posh council-house friend (who was the proud owner of a Timex watch) as I hurtled along the imaginary touchline, about to lay the ball in the path of the imaginary Billy Liddell, which he would run onto and blast one of his thunderbolts past an imaginary immobile Jimmy O'Neill, the Everton goalkeeper. Then Billy would turn and run towards me with a big beam on his face, his hand outstretched to shake mine and selflessly congratulate me for 'making' the goal. In truth my pass would have been either too short or too long, for in reality I have always made short or long passes through all of life's attempts on goal, never a perfect one, but nonetheless have managed to survive well into the second half with a couple of injuries but without being substituted.

There was an upturn in our living arrangements after the departure of my grandmother. My brother and I had a bedroom to share: what had been my grandmother's living room became our living room and the so-called kitchen became the dining room. The back kitchen became my mother's sole occupancy for the first time and the Victorian range was dismantled. Electricity, which until then had only been installed in the lighting circuit, became available through two wall sockets. We invested in a second-hand electric iron which was easier than keeping two flat irons and heating them on the gas ring. The fault-line became more indistinct, although the cracks were ever-present. By this time Algy had gone to meet his maker and betting shops became licensed, much to the heartfelt approval of my father.

Power from a light socket caused a near-death experience for my brother. In an effort to alleviate the effects of cold and damp in our beds, my father constructed a 'bed warmer' which consisted of a long length of cable with a light socket plug on one end and a light socket at the other. Other people would have bought hot-water bottles. The end with the light socket was fed through a biscuit tin with a hole cut into it and then a bulb was plugged in. Hey presto! A modern version of a bed warmer, powered by the heat from a light bulb as opposed to hot coals. It worked, but was dismantled after my brother decided to investigate its construction and it went off with an enormous flash, fusing the lights and discharging a pungent smell of burning rubber.

My father, who possessed the ingenuity to strip and assemble a Rolls Royce, was a man of surprising and novel inventiveness when it came to matters mechanical or electrical. When I was about eight years old I was walking with him in South Road when we came across a broken-down Austin Seven with a policeman under the bonnet trying to get it started. He just couldn't help himself, and without even a nod of introduction he elbowed the policeman away and poked his head in.

> "What's the matter with it?"
>
> "I don't know. It just won't start and the battery is dead".
>
> "No wonder it won't bloody well start, you've flooded it! You wouldn't be able to start if you were drowned, would you?"

I cringed, believing that an arrest was imminent.

> "Get the bloody starting handle and give it a turn, and be careful you don't break your bloody thumbs."

The policeman was a very big man, and he pulled himself up to his full height with a quizzical expression on his face.

> "I've seen you, haven't I? You drive a hearse. You'd better be careful or you'll find yourself in the back compartment with somebody else driving YOU."

*"Just bloody well do it and you'll be on your way.
Give her a turn and she'll go nice as ninepence."*

The policemen did as he was told, the engine jumped into life, his thumbs remained intact, and he was on his way with a face like an Easter Island statue.

*"Bloody self-starters! If they hadn't been invented
none of them would ever be able to get out of a
bloody garage."*

I had no idea what he was talking about. I was just relieved that the incident had drawn to a satisfactory conclusion. This was a man who could catch a fish with a bent pin and extinguish an incendiary bomb, but could never back a winner, or so he said. This lie was uncovered several years later, when my mother was returning washed socks to a drawer. Underneath some clothing she discovered a cache of brown pay-packets which had never been opened. It turned out that he had had a major win of a couple of hundred pounds, and for a several months had been using this money for housekeeping and as further ammunition to gamble with.

My mother died young; her last live foray into the street was witnessed by neighbours who noticed her clinging to a set of railings as she was limping towards the bookmaker's office to lay a bet on for my father who was 'not well enough' to get there himself. The next day, at the age of sixty-eight, she died and he cried. He, on the other hand, lived on until nearly ninety, still advising long-suffering residents in a care home on what and what not to do. He called himself the Head Boy, harangued the staff into giving him his own door key, encouraged a squawking seagull to visit every morning by feeding it lumps of Spam from sandwiches provided by his carers *("I've never eaten bloody Spam in my life, and I'm not going to bloody well start now"),* built a putting green in the grounds – but no-one would play with him – and made an irascible irritant of himself in the local pub by insisting on being the 'pot man' in return for gin and tonic. The volume on his portable television was so loud that when he was shouting at the horses running sideways it could be heard from the houses next door. There were complaints. *"They wouldn't hear anything if they shut their bloody windows"* he said. His hearing aid whistled constantly even when switched off, because he had taken it to pieces to see how it worked, and so confusion reigned among the plethora of misunderstood conversations.

One of his more novel inventions in the dusk of his years was a contraption he called his 'suspender belt', consisting of a pair of braces which he had refashioned to fit around his waist to hold up the elastic stockings that supported his varicose veins. It was confiscated. Likewise a pair of tights, which he wore on his head to keep it warm at night. Speculation among residents in the home that he was a transvestite incensed him. All that he left was a newspaper bill for the *Sporting Life* and an account from the betting shop for £17.00. I still cannot comprehend how this man with no formal education at all actually produced a blueprint for a rotary engine which preceded the Wankel pistonless engine first patented in 1929, and yet never had the forethought or inclination to patent this work himself.

> *"All that bloody nonsense to make wheels go around*
> *by pushing pistons up and down. More corners than*
> *a bag of nails. All they are doing is losing power that*
> *should go straight to the crankshaft".*

If I had not seen it, I would not have believed it.

My father applied lateral thinking to his inventions. He devised an unusual but effective contraption for trapping and killing mice by using a bowl of water and a strip of wood, with one end positioned on the floor up against its rim and the other end of it overhanging the middle of the bowl with a piece of cheese attached to it. The unwitting mouse was tempted to climb up the wooden strip in a vain quest to liberate the cheese, but before it could seize it, the mouse was tipped into the water.

*

When my turn came, I didn't get to the grammar school. I hadn't taken any interest in the adventures of Biggles. The *Dandy* was not required reading, drawing of cowboy hats was not considered art, and interminably kicking a football against a wall instead of learning my tables conspired against my intellectual potential to the extent that on the day of the exam, which happened to be a Saturday, I was in a jam. My school was a mere fifty yards from the Odeon cinema, and Flash Gordon was featuring that day in an episode relating to the on-going saga of the rock men who spoke backwards and whose main purpose in life was to keep clear of the giant lizards by camouflaging themselves in canvas suits painted grey, thus enabling them to blend in with the rocks. And I had sixpence. So I decided to sit the exam and then pop into the Odeon on my way home. I did sit the exam for about half an hour, and then in I popped to the Odeon just in time catch the scene where Professor Zarkov, Flash Gordon's bearded intrepid companion and adviser on all matters scientific, manages to translate the language of the rock men because of his knowledge of their ancient ancestry which originated thousands of years ago in the Gobi desert. He had studied their language and he also could speak backwards.

Nobody seemed too concerned that I did not go to the grammar school; in fact it was a foregone unspoken conclusion. My father assured my mother that my bloody brain was in my bloody boots. My brother was relieved that I would not be tagging along with him, and I was content in the knowledge that I would not have to go to school on Saturday mornings, and could therefore continue my usual Saturday morning football training of kicking the ball against the now well-battered doors of the Lion and Unicorn, and then of following the exploits of Flash Gordon, Hopalong Cassidy with Topper his horse and bewhiskered toothless sidekick Gabby Hayes, Abbott and Costello, and Zorro.

I was shunted over the railings and into the real big boys' secondary modern school, to continue my faltering educational experience and to face the wrath of Gotch, which didn't occur. The axiom *don't worry, it may never happen* was never more apposite. He taught history and I overheard him talking about the Jacobites to another teacher one day. They seemed as alien to me as the rock men; my brains resided in my boots. It also turned out that he was an extremely mild man whose countenance, although not sunny, was not true his nature.

Sums, reading and writing were a more necessary requirement for my intellectual advancement; not maths, literature and composition. What I encountered at my secondary school were more songs which didn't really add up, although an attempt was made to teach me to add up which was not very successful and on occasions resulted in a sharp slap across my knuckles with the edge of a ruler, administered forcefully by a bunioned spinster known as who Ma Stick. A little ferret of a woman ostensibly taught geography by having us recite the names of the Liverpool docks, no doubt in an attempt to point us in the direction of where to go to find a job. She seemed to set great store by having us delve into the wealth of the great British Empire via a textbook which displayed all the produce from around the Empire that was transported to Liverpool. It also displayed line drawings and grainy photographs of black people called 'savages' who inhabited some of these far-off countries, and who had not yet been 'Christianised'. During her time as my tutor in colonial xenophobia, I had suffered a further broken arm via a push in the back while leaping to head a tennis ball in a game of football in the schoolyard, and it was this teacher who described my writing as 'infantile' after forcing me to write with my left hand while my right arm was suspended in a sling for six weeks.

And then there was Woan. Until very recently, he lived simultaneously in both a literal and a metaphoric gothic tower as retired organist and choirmaster of Liverpool's Anglican Cathedral, feted by many but despised by me for sinking almost to the level of the midget, not because of the daft unintelligible songs he had us sing but because he actually broke my treasured copy of Elvis Presley's *Hound Dog*.

"This is NOT, nor ever will it be, music."

Justification for my resentment came recently from the disclosure that this man was such an iconoclast that at the same time as he was maligning Elvis Presley, he could not recognise that the young Paul McCartney's voice was destined for far more musical acclaim than he would ever aspire to; he judged him to be unacceptable as a chorister for his cathedral choir. There was another occasion when this man unjustifiably – and with some measure of malice – marched me by the ear to the headmaster through the battlefield/playground, much to the relieved amusement of the hooligan who had thrown a banger into the music room.

Mr Riddick was a headmaster who caned serious miscreants in front of the whole school. Other children whose crimes were not so serious were not humiliated in such fashion, but nonetheless caned in his office, or so I – and Woan – believed. The truth of the matter is that Stanley Riddick was a man who knew full well the quality of mercy. Although a stern advocate of corporal punishment, he was not without restraint in such matters.

> *"Mr Riddick, I want you to cane this boy. He has just thrown a firework into my room."*

Riddick was a tall slim man with a kindly face and a gentle manner, regardless of instilling discipline with ferocity when he believed necessary. He eyed me from a great height and detected the quiver of my lower lip. He then looked at Woan and back to me.

> *"Well, what have you got to say about this, boy?"*
> *"It wasn't me sir, I didn't do it."*
> *"Well then, who did do it?"*
> *"I don't know sir."*
> *"But you were there?"*
> *"Yes sir, but I didn't do it."*
> *"Well who did?"*
> *"I don't know sir, but I didn't do it."*

Woan primed himself for a verbal onslaught.

> *"I know this boy Mr Riddick. He's a trouble maker, and he copies other people's work. He's always kicking balls against windows."*

This was untrue. I had not copied anything. Everyone compared notes when Woan was otherwise engaged with the intricacies of a gramophone, upon which he would play *The Duke of Plaza Toro* and *While we were Marching through Georgia* or some similar jingoistic songs, and upon which my recording of *Hound Dog* came to such a violent end. The way I saw things was that to compare was not to copy. The notes I was alleged to have copied were in fact musical notes – crotchets, quavers, and minims with which I was already acquainted through my induction into the church choir.

> *"I've also seen him on the dinner hut roof throwing lumps of coke at the Merchant Taylors' boys."*

This regular early-morning pursuit of making the kids who wore straw boaters run the gauntlet through a hail of cinders on the way to their exclusive school half a mile further down Crosby Road was not unknown to me, although I had only been on the roof once and that was to retrieve my treasured football which had landed there because of a toe-ender, the like of which Algy had painstakingly instructed me not to do. At this final nail in the coffin of a twelve-year-old, exceedingly misunderstood child instilled with the upright fibre of the great Billy Liddell, Mr Riddick nodded gravely to Woan, although I discerned the slight intimation of a smile.

> *"Thank you Mr Woan. Leave him here with me, and I will do what is necessary."*

Woan left me to my fate, although I was unaware of his footsteps fading along the corridor.

Stanley Riddick looked at me perceptively, no doubt noting the scuffed shoes and muddy scabbed knees.

> *"Well, you cannot deny that you spend a lot of time kicking a football, can you?"*

Then something totally unforeseen occurred. He reached into the oak glass-fronted bookcase and took a cane out. I began to shake, and he began to smile. He put his finger to his lips, slowly shook his head from side to side looking at the closed door and with a conspiratorial wink proceeded to give six smacks to one of the leather arms of his chair. He then winked at me again and pointed towards the door. As I left the headmaster's study, through the haze of my welled-up watering eyes, I thought I just caught sight of Woan disappearing around the corner of the corridor.

The outcome of this encounter greatly enhanced my reputation among my footballing contemporaries, one of whom was the banger thrower, a boy whose ability I would have given everything for, and who had flattened me when I was trying to head a tennis ball. He didn't even own a pair of football boots, so I willingly lent him my prized rugby boots when he was selected to play for Lancashire Schoolboys. This was no mean sacrifice, but Fairclough was something special. What he could do with a tennis ball at his feet had to be seen to be believed. The great sadness was that he treated this natural ingenious talent with disdain. Some years later I met him carrying our dustbin out to a cart. He seemed happy in his work, although when talking to him he told me that he had been signed as an apprentice at Everton, but gave it up because part of the job was to clean the boots of the first team players. I would have willingly cleaned the boots of the groundsman for such an opportunity, even if it was Everton's groundsman.

Just when you think the ball has crossed the line
  It curves, and back it comes again
  Relief is stung by grief
  When you find
  You are offside
  Once more

7

THE SPION KOP

*"Behind a paper-strewn desk high in Liverpool
University Students' Union building, two famous
feet twitched. Feet that belonged to the original,
uncrowned king of football lore – Billy Liddell. Feet
of power and romance that longed for the old days as
their owner reflected on past affairs of plunder.*

*"It is said that when Liddell called at the Anfield
ground one day last year – five years after the close of
his career – work stopped on the new stand that was
being built. 'There's Billy Liddell', a navvy gasped.
To a man they removed their industrial helmets,
clutched them reverently to their waists and bowed
their heads. The old master was passing through."*

30 November 1966 – from *Sunday Express*

Billy Liddell imparted life skills by shining example. Do not
give up. Never be afraid of trying. If you are knocked down,
don't stay down unless you are unconscious. Never cheat.
Be generous in your applause for a worthy rival. Of course he never
said these things; he exemplified them by his own actions. The myths
about him which circulated in my generation were not myths at all.
He *did* break a crossbar with a powerful shot. He *did* burst a ball
with a blistering header. He *did* burst the net. He *did* fracture the
arm of a goalkeeper with a shot from a free kick. He *did* plead with
the referee not to send a player off the field for a violently brutal

attack on him, and he won this strange yet gracious appeal. Unlike his legions of fans he never swore, and he was respected because of it – not for being a pedant but for his self-control. He didn't drink alcohol and yet he never reproached others for doing so. He never committed a foul on purpose. He ran a boys' club and was a magistrate. He became bursar of Liverpool University. He walked on water, and he epitomised everything that should be taught by example and not learned by repetitious written rules.

The first time I saw him play was at Anfield when I was eleven. Liverpool was a second division team then and the opposition was Grimsby Town. My father took me – not into the famous Spion Kop (named after the disgraceful shambles of the Boer War battle) which would cram over 27,000 supporters into its roaring cavernous hooded vault behind the goal which, from the upper terraces, resembled matchsticks with the players like marauding red ants – but into the lesser chaotic seated area known as the paddock. The swaying ocean of red and white and the wonder of so many men shouting with one voice 'GIVE IT TO LIDDELL' sent a shiver down my young spine. Then came the thunderous roar and the clattering of thousands of wooden red-and-white rattles when the ball was passed to Billy to do his best with. He always did his best. He never, ever, let them down. His spirit survives in the adopted anthem which is bawled out by thousands and thousands all over the world – *You'll Never Walk Alone.* Bill Shankly, the world's legendary ambassador of football-speak who managed Liverpool during the glowing embers of Billy's career, called him his personal Exocet. Like me, hundreds of boys were transported to a level of understanding of the game of football and of life which surpasses the on-field battle. Shankly embodied this notion in his famous oft-quoted proclamation that football isn't a matter of life and death; it is much more serious than that.

Another less celebrated Shanklyism rings true for me: *Me having no education – I had to use my brains.* School was a place I went to for sums and spelling; Anfield was a college of knowledge and enlightenment. Good manners were more than holding a knife and fork in a way which conformed to social principles. Good manners were the practical concern for your fellow beings, no matter how improper in polite society. Good manners, inspired by the example of Billy, were to applaud the opposition off the field if they managed to win a match at Anfield. The call of *Roll up yer footie Echo wack,* from a burly docker replete with three chins and a broken nose, is a case in point. What do you do in a crowd of fifty thousand when you want to pee? You roll up a newspaper and pee through it vertically to avoid splashing anybody. If one was too short to see the game, another supporter would lend his lunch box for him to stand on and his shoulder to lean on. Boys were transported over the heads of men down to the front of the terraces for a close-up view of the Liddell magic, and were told by rough, unkempt dockers *Dat's da way to do it lar,* when Billy came charging through. Often when he scored a goal into the Kop end he would turn, not to the deafening thunderous roar of the crowd to crow his achievement, but to the opposing defeated goalkeeper to pat him on the shoulder and console him in a display of generous and genuine sympathy, as if to say *you tried, and you can do no more than try.*

Short of Jesus Christ Almighty, who could be a better example to a child growing up on a fault-line of how to live life, regardless of our personal frailties? *To be a Pilgrim* just didn't ring my bell. Baden-Powell's boy scouts were a force to be reckoned with, but the power, humility and all-embracing togetherness fostered by Liddell on the Kop were unsurpassable. Life, with all its fragilities, burdens and unforeseeable future, was welded together by a thread of euphoric excitement and played out in front of my enchanted eyes, in an arena where Christians were never fed to the lions and war never killed anyone. Romantic idealism from a twelve-year-old who would rather kick a ball than go to school and who couldn't figure out long division, but could instinctively judge the trajectory needed to take an in-swinging corner kick and place it on the head of the magnificent Billy Liddell? I'll say!

And so, from the age of twelve, I spent many Saturday afternoons on the Kop venerating my champion and honouring his inspired and talented capacity for kicking and heading a ball, alongside tens of thousands of like-minded enthusiasts for the game which was more than just a game. From behind the Kop goalmouth, I had a ringside view before the match of the antics of the Walrus, a beefy bluff red-faced policeman with a bushy moustache and bugger's grips, waving his stick at the sprightly little grizzled old man in an even older overcoat dribbling a tennis ball into the penalty area and deftly side-footing it into the empty goal. I would join in the eruption of euphoric delight emanating from thousands of men-boys as the little old man scored a symbolic goal, retrieved his ball and raced off the pitch, to be swallowed up by the delighted crowd, followed by the lumbering puffing Walrus shaking his stick at all and sundry, blowing out his cheeks in a mock display of authoritative fury. Then, added to this this dramatic burlesque of fury would come the chant resounding throughout the Kop – "THE WALRUS, THE WALRUS, THE WALRUS, THE WALRUS!" I had never knowingly read a word of Shakespeare until I was seventeen, yet here before my innocent eyes stood his play within a play, the dumb show, before my Hamlet in the form of Billy Liddell had even set foot on the field. Shakespeare was not on the school curriculum for me, but I didn't miss out because the essence of his magnificence was suffused at Anfield, and the genius for the descriptive power of the English language was also present in the unschooled, but resplendently imaginative, usage of defamiliarising metaphor as a means of displaying the essence of euphoria:

> *"Der wuz der fukin arms in der, der wuz der fukin legs in der, der wuz der whole fukin bodees in der."*

Quote from an ecstatic fan
describing a goalmouth scramble.

I touched Billy Liddell. What's more, he even spoke to me. I was given permission to travel to Blackburn with a coachload of fanatics to see my team play, and play they did. The final score was a 3 – 3 draw. I was present when Billy scored all three of Liverpool's goals in what was regarded as the finest hat-trick of the century. One with the left foot, one with the right, and one with the head. This is a fact – one of his shots was so hard that it left four men on the ground before it scorched the net, and the goalkeeper hadn't moved a muscle. The *Liverpool Echo* confirmed what I and a cohort of demented red-and-white followers had seen.

At the final whistle I couldn't resist the exhilarating temptation of nipping over the wall and onto the pitch in a mad dash to catch up with Billy and pat him on the back of his famous muddied number nine shirt before he disappeared into the players' tunnel. I managed it, but with unforeseen bittersweet consequences. Almost instantaneously I saw stars and for a second wobbled before I felt the sting of a blow to the back of my head, not unlike the pain experienced when walking backwards into lampposts.

"Geroutofit, and don't come back!"

A policeman, far less substantial in stature compared to the Walrus and of a much less sunny disposition, was confronting me with an arm raised to deliver a further blow. The prodigious Billy Liddell turned in his tracks to face us and spoke in the mildest of tones to the blustering Blackburn bobby.

*"There's no need to be so harsh with the lad. He's
done no harm and he's only showing his happiness,
and what's so bad about a child being happy?"*

That said it all. The policeman faded away, and Billy Liddell looked down at me.

*"You must not do this again sonny. Now get off home
with you, there's a good lad."*

In a flash he was gone, and I was left dazed from the blow to my head, but even more so by the fact that Billy Liddell had spoken to Georgie Porter, the next best thing to passing the ball to him.

*There is no drama in a play
Only parody sustained by reality
It cannot be taught
It can only be lived.*

8

SCOUTING FOR MEN

There is no real doubt that strong motivation for the Scouts was the preparation of British men for military service ...

I fell for that, hook line and sinker.

From the age of twelve I became conscious, through my initiation into the Boy Scouts movement, of my social and educational frailties. Most of the budding adolescents I became acquainted with were from the more stable side of the fault-line, and I began to feel uncomfortable about my own background and scholastic inadequacy, especially when taking part in the many activities associated with this undercover military recruitment organisation for working-class boys. It had been instituted by a celebrated national hero who, I later learned, was little more than an imperialist degenerate aristocrat in fancy dress with a self-confessed partiality for photographs of naked boys and an abhorrence of the female form, and who declared that *Mien Kampf* was a "wonderful book with good ideas on education, health, propaganda and organisation." Of course I was unaware of this at the time, although I did think it was a bit odd that fully grown men walked the streets in this strange paramilitary garb of shorts, green garter tags, a neckerchief which in an emergency could be used as a sling, a tourniquet or a head bandage, held together by something called a woggle and a strange russet hat faintly reminiscent of the one worn by Roy Rogers. It was just about acceptable for boys to go about dressed like this (unless they came up against the likes of Yocker Spencer), but *grown men?* And to this day I have never heard of anyone using a boy scout's neckerchief as a sling, a tourniquet or a head bandage.

In *Scouting For Boys*, Baden-Powell's definitive and multi-million selling textbook on matters relating to adolescent development, and his theory that boys should be trained to be good citizens by living a life as close to tribal mores as possible, there was a passage, now abridged, relating to "beastliness", the remedy for which, if one suffers an attack, is a cold shower. I had no idea what this man was referring to. I thought it may have something to do with the cat. Taking account of the sort of unsavoury circles this venerated warrior moved in when visiting his old public school, with his repugnant penchant for poring over photographs of naked boys with his old headmaster, or possibly even his over-familiarity with a junior officer in his regiment he always referred to wistfully as his "boy"; he must have spent many fraught hours having cold showers. I certainly was not going to ask my mother what beastliness was, for even though I was developing, the airborne slipper had not yet become a distant memory. Besides, although we had plenty of cold water to wash in, we didn't have a shower. I did ask my scoutmaster, a pious and cheerless individual with a love of singing daft gibberish songs – *Ging Gang Goolie Goolie* (penned by Baden-Powell himself) being one – but he just went red and told me I would learn all about it when I was older.

Of course, in common with many of the boys of the Hitler Youth, an organisation which Baden-Powell is on record as admiring in the months before the war, even fostering an exchange visit, I was ideal potential fodder for future military service. I was a serious contender for scouting success as a patrol leader with my khaki shirt festooned in badges and was on course to achieve my Bushman's Thong to be worn around my shoulder, not knowing then or now what it was or is, but was unable to vault a five-bar gate, thus negating my probability of winning such an award. I believed that my lack of formal education would be no major impediment to joining the military. The noble ideas on health, propaganda and organisation so blatantly declared in BP's manifesto was music to the ears of a recruiting officer aiming his sights at thirteen-year-old working-class boys with scant education and little prospect of progress in any other field. There was I, waiting to be hooked, and what better periodical could there be to advertise this imperialist propaganda than *The Eagle*? So it was goodbye to Korky the Cat and Freddy the Fly, and hello to Digby, PC 49 and The Mekon – a very tame adversary in comparison to Ming the Merciless.

It went unheeded that a comic aimed at young boys was able to display large advertisements on behalf of the Army for the enlistment of boy soldiers for a term of twelve years. Weaponry in the form of air pistols, rifles, aluminium catapults and knives were also advertised on facing pages which were conveniently placed to further the emergent warrior instincts characteristic among many developing boys. The advertisement that registered with me and many contemporaries – apart from those who had been pressed into twelve years' service by toadying magistrates as an alternative to Borstal, to the pleasure of the armed forces recruitment controllers – was one which showed a grinning freckle-faced boy swinging across a river dangling from a rope, with a weapon, dressed as a warrior and having fun while presenting an image of a wholesome youth "doing his duty for God and the Queen" as the scout promise articulated it. When I was just thirteen years old, my mind was made up. I was going to be a soldier and continue my scouting activities in a manner which would give me kudos and mitigate to some extent my problematic lack of education. I would be able to swing across rivers on a rope and kick footballs unimpeded. I would shoot guns. I would obtain prestige. My father who, because of his health had never served in the armed forces although he lost two brothers in the Great War, was elated when I told him of my plans for the future.

> *"Three square meals a day. See the world. Make a bloody man of you. They'll make you straighten your back and walk forwards."*

He could have added to this response that I would be one less mouth to feed, although he did say that just because I was going to join the army, it didn't mean that I was not going to send any money home. A boy soldier's pay at the time was the equivalent of seventy-five pence per week. Subtract from that the cost of Blanco, boot polish, Brasso, dusters, toothpaste and the odd pork pie to stave off hunger pangs, there wasn't a great deal left to send home. The reference to walking forwards was disingenuous, because I had stopped walking backwards by the age of eight. My mother appeared less enthusiastic about the notion of her Georgie with a gun in his hands, and my brother scoffed. He declared himself a pacifist the nearer the time came for him to be conscripted, which by a fluke of circumstance relating to his date of birth, he managed to avoid. Nevertheless, humiliation of a most disconcerting kind lay salivating for him in the wings.

There was a problem with my military aspirations because I was still a schoolboy and unable to leave school before the age of fifteen. The recruiting sergeant seemed unconcerned and filled in my paperwork stating that my current employment was 'scholar', and told me to approach my Headmaster with a view to leaving school as soon as possible, because boy soldiers still have to study anyway: what I discovered when I eventually joined my unit was not exactly Janet and John again, but not a great deal remote from them. Stanley Riddick was persuaded – probably because he was, I believe, a retired army officer and because I was unlikely to advance any further beyond my twelve times table and nouns and adjectives – that I could leave school when I was fourteen, so I completed my schooling some six months before I was finally enlisted.

*

Meanwhile, my brother had finished his education in a haphazard manner, for although he went to the grammar school, residing on the fault-line was still a sociological burden. He was, to my mind, growing stranger by the day. He had taken wearing his V-neck pullover back to front under his jacket, wearing horn-rimmed spectacles without any lenses in them, and listening to traditional jazz when Elvis was blaring out everywhere else. This was in the pre-Beatles era, when Kenny Ball and his Paramount Jazz Band were pulling young punters in at the Cavern wearing their pullovers back to front and being 'sent'. To say that my brother scorned Elvis Presley would be an understatement. Woan would have been impressed. He had also acquired a set of bongo drums, and a small camera with which to capture arty-farty pictures of the cat, whereas my personal accessories consisted of an air rifle, an untunable battered guitar with two strings missing, and an autograph book containing Billy

Liddell's copperplate signature alongside the scribbled mark of the Flying Pig – Tommy Lawrence, Liverpool's elephantine airborne goalkeeper. The air rifle was bought from a secondhand shop with savings from my milk round from which I'd recently been fired because milk was appearing on the wrong doorsteps due to genuine misunderstandings of a geographical nature. I tried to explain the full picture to the gruff proprietor of the dairy, but he would not listen.

> *"Bugger off and don't come back. If this carries on I'll be ruined. And you've been nickin' the orange juice, so I'll knock that off your wages."*

This was a slur. In point of fact I had accidentally dropped a metal basket containing six bottles when I tripped over a kerbstone. I thought it wise not to make a clean breast of it, coming as it did so soon after the incident in which my extremely overladen and wobbly-wheeled handcart came into contact with the rear end of a stationary Ford Anglia parked on a downward slope in the road at five o'clock one Sunday morning, giving rise to an early start to the day for the local residents.

The air rifle had become a matter of considerable distress to my mother and foreboding to my father.

> *"You can get rid of that bloody thing before you put somebody's bloody eye out with it."*

Of course, he was right. The thought of a fourteen-year-old with delusions of becoming a frontline warrior in possession of such a weapon says a great deal about my mind-set at the time. Our decaying home also began to suffer a further burden when the cracked ceiling began to develop pockmarks, due to the numerous pellets embedded in the plaster, many of which contained the gory remnants of slaughtered flies. My protestations that I was decimating the fly population to the betterment of our health went unheeded.

"If you have still got that bloody thing in the house
when I come home tomorrow I'll break it to bloody
pieces, army or no bloody army!"

So I traded it in for a threadbare tennis racquet in the doubtful
optimism that I might be able to inveigle my way into the company
of Janet Watson, a thirteen-year-old siren who regularly played
tennis in the park. However, this was not to be. Not only did she
belittle my service, which often seemed to go sideways over the
fence in the same way as my toe-enders went over the bar, but she
had a boyfriend who took every opportunity to blast his tennis balls
at my abdomen.

My brother had meanwhile become a potential high-flyer in
the bakery and grocery industry, where he was earmarked as future
management potential by Thomas Scott's Bakery – *the home of good
bread* – a family-run concern that was well established throughout
the Liverpool suburbs. And this is where our paths crossed.

Since I had finished school six months before enlistment, full-
time employment was considered necessary, although impossible
to acquire for several reasons, the prime ones being that I was
under age and I still couldn't do my twelve times table. What's
more, most full-time work required attendance on Saturdays, and
this would greatly interfere with my football fixation. Nevertheless,
after many fruitless evenings looking through the vacancies column
in the *Liverpool Echo* for a potential employer, the difficulty was
overcome – for me at least. But for my brother, with his reverse
pullover, traditional jazz, glassless spectacles, bongo banging and
cat photography, things were not so rosy, for it was he who was
harassed by my parents into arranging an interview for me for a job
in the grocery trade. This was a definite boon, especially with my
knowledge of the dairy industry, yet for him a situation of grave
injustice and severe embarrassment. We had never seen eye to eye,
my brother and me, and this intrusion into his personal sphere of
employment could not have helped matters, me being – in his eyes
– little more than pond life.

And so I attended the head office of Scott's Bakery for the first
interview of my working life. A cheery little man, rather rotund with

black slicked-back receding hair, rosy cheeks and an appropriate blob of dough for a nose, was the person who would decide my future career path. I noticed he was wearing an Everton FC badge in his lapel and a blue tie, both of which caused a certain degree of trepidation before I had even spoken.

"Don't just stand there son, take a seat, I won't bite."

He seemed a jolly person, and this surprised me, considering the fact that he was wearing the blue-and-white emblem of the left-footer rock cakes, terms of derision for Evertonians which I had heard from some Liverpool supporters but had no idea what they meant. I now know that a rock cake is abusive terminology for a Roman Catholic, and likewise a left-footer is so called because it was believed that Irish Catholic labourers used their left foot to push a spade into the ground, whereas Protestants used their right foot.

"Now, you're Michael's young brother, aren't you? A bright lad is Michael; he'll go a long way."
"Yes sir."
"Are you as bright as him?
"Yes sir."

The first lie of what was to be many through the years of interviews and consultations, tripped off my juvenile tongue with brazen alacrity, and the second one followed in swift succession.

"How old are you, George?"
"Fifteen sir."

The second lie was tangible, but the first was open to enquiry, and enquire into my audacious assertion that I was as bright as my brother he did.

"Tell me George, what do threepence halfpenny and two shillings and sixpence halfpenny make?"

I was struck dumb. This was an unexpected assault on my mental arithmetic skills, which had been severely challenged by Ma Stick in the past. I wasn't expecting to be required to add up – especially with fractions involved. I looked to the ceiling as though I was pondering a correct reply, but after about half a minute, which seemed to me to be more like an hour, my interrogator spoke.

"Go on son, have a bash."

He was beaming at me – almost willing me to endorse my lie that my ability in such matters was on a par with my elder sibling. So a bash I had.

"Three shillings."

He looked at me with an amused glint in his eye.

"No, I'm afraid that's not right, but if you carry on like that if we take you on you will certainly increase our profits."

Then came the clincher – the third lie. The lie that got me the job and shamed me at the expense of being assessed as fit for employment by Scott's Bakery.

"What are you – red or blue? Liverpool or Everton?"
"Blue sir – Everton."

I swallowed hard and tried to look relaxed about the remark, trusting that if I was believed the interview would come to a successful conclusion and I would be accepted into the grocery trade. But this was a merely preliminary question, generalising my inquisitor's overall interest in my football-supporting allegiance.

"Who's your favourite player?"

Davey Hickson was berated and scorned by every Liverpool supporter as the lowest form of animal ever to have set foot on a football pitch, and who would be capable of breaking his own granny's legs if he were to intercept her in the penalty area. The great irony is that – not much later in his career – he was transferred to Liverpool from Everton, and the famous Kop choir changed its tuneful venom about him being born in a chimney-stack in Ellesmere Port into songs of unrestrained praise.

"Davey Hickson sir."

(Verily I say unto thee, that this day ... before the cock crow twice thou shalt deny me thrice.
Gospel according to St Mark 14.30)

There! I'd said it. Surely I was home and dry. He nearly fell off his seat, and I felt bilious.

"Good lad! He's the man to stop Liddell's prancing isn't he? Doesn't get a look in when Davey's on his case. You've got the job and you can start on Monday in our shop in South Road."

Consider speech.
Every uttered word was born and weaned
To clarify thoughts inherent yet unspeakable
Thoughts of truth.
Yet substitute word with well-found word
And lies are brought into the world

9

"OUR LOSS IS RUSSIA'S GAIN"

S o there I was, making an entrance on a cheery bright Monday morning into the world of tinned salmon and crusty cobs. I couldn't wait for payday.

> *"You're Georgie Porter aren't you? We know you,*
> *don't we? You used to come telling us to mend our*
> *broken biscuits, didn't you? We know your mother,*
> *don't we? Your brother is Michael isn't he?"*

Two harpiesque ladies gazed out from the counter at me as I sauntered into our local Scott's branch trying to look nonchalant. They were both wearing conspiratorial smiles that cracked their war-paint, which might well have been mortared on with a small trowel. The scarlet lipstick coating on the lips of one of them had invaded her upper front teeth, and the other older lady had gone to futile lengths in an attempt to avoid her lipstick running into the fissures around her lips.

> *"Oo 'eez a nice lad, isn't 'ee Mabel?"*
> *"Yes 'ee is that Edna, isn' 'ee? I remember 'im in short*
> *pants, don't I? Old Jack used to see 'im over the road,*
> *didn' 'ee?"*

These people conversed in questions. Mabel, the older of the two with corrugated bright orange hair, was in charge. She told me she was the manageress and I was to help her in the shop. She smiled benignly down at me from over a bacon slicer with a great big wheel and a handle on it that turned the blade, her double chin highlighted by the glare reflected onto her face from the big shiny wheel.

"I've been given me orders from 'ead office, 'aven't I luv? I was told you are not to use the till until I am sure you can add up, wasn't I luv? You can't use the bacon slicer either, can you luv? But I've been told you can slice the corned beef with a knife, 'aven't I luv? And you 'ave got to be careful of the trap door, 'aven't you luv?"

Was this a wind up, or was there really a trap door? Indeed there was. It was located behind the cake and biscuit counter, and some steep wooden steps led down to a basement where stock was held and all the necessary devices for making tea and coffee for the staff. It looked quite cosy from above.

I survived just one day at that branch of Scott's. I hadn't even served a customer. I had just put on my new white nylon overall and had done what I thought was a reasonable job mopping the floor. I continued the process behind the counter, mopping and walking backwards along the floor. The inevitable outcome did not dawn on me for what must have been two or three seconds when I found myself on the floor of the basement alongside a large wooden tray of squashed custard tarts which had broken my fall. Two alarmed and very concerned ladies were peering down at me. Concerned not for me, however.

"I told 'im Edna, I told 'im didn't I? Didn't I tell 'im to be careful of the trap door? Yo 'eard me didn't you Edna, you 'eard me tel l'im, didn't you? I'm not taking the blame for this, am I?"

"Oh yes Mabel, oh yes, I 'eard you, didn't I? 'Ee was walking backwards, wasn't 'ee? Look at all those custard tarts everywhere; what are we going to do

*with them? There'll 'ave to be a stock check, won't
there? I used to see 'im walking backwards when 'ee
was little, didn't I?"*

Up to this juncture, neither of them had enquired about
my wellbeing. I attempted to struggle to my feet with one hand
embedded in the remains of a custard tart and my new nylon overall
spattered with custard and flakes of pastry adhered to it, and slipped
on another, exacerbating the situation by grabbing at a table leg and
tipping a plate of Swiss rolls into the quagmire.

> *"Look what 'ees done now Mabel, can you see what
> 'ees done now? 'Ees tipped our lunch over, hasn't 'ee?
> What are we going to do Mabel, what are we going to
> do?"*
> *"We'd better phone 'ead office, 'adn't we? Are you
> alright Georgie luv? You aven't broke your arm again
> 'av you luv? Your mother'll go mad if you 'av, won't
> she luv?"*

How did this person know that I had broken my arm on several
occasions? Also, a question which had been at the back of my mind
for some time suddenly came to the fore. How did my mother know
that I had been into this shop many times while keeping my sunny
side up suggesting that broken biscuits should be mended? The
answer was gawping down on me from above, hands on ample hips,
shamelessly displaying a pair of voluminous navy-blue bloomers,
elasticated just above her knees. This was a garment I thought only
Martha wore.

A customer appeared in the middle of this mayhem and was
ushered brusquely out of the door, which was hastily shut and the
closed sign was put up. I heard one half of a stilted conversation
being conducted on the telephone.

> *"It wasn't our fault, was it? ....we can't keep 'im 'ere,
> can we? ... 'eel kill 'imself, won't 'ee? ... what about*

all those custard tarts? ... right ... .right... right ...
right ... well, 'ee can start there tomorrow, can 't 'ee?
... don 't tell them what happened though, or they won 't
take 'im, will they? ... 'Ee's Michael's brother, isn 't
'ee? "

The solution to the ladies' dilemma was solved by moving me to another branch without a trap door and swapping the tray of damaged custard tarts for another when the delivery van arrived. So we cleared the mess up, dumped it all back in the big wooden tray, and calmed our nerves by having a brew-up and a bun. I was then sent home and told to report the following day to the Mount Pleasant branch about half a mile away. And so I did.

*

At the second posting, things seemed to be swimming along nicely. I was a very willing worker when it came to sweeping up, mopping the street in the front of the shop, making coffee, pulling down the sunblind with a long pole and helping the man delivering supplies from the van. Things started to go a bit wobbly after about two weeks when I was given the responsibility of writing the day's special offers in whitewash on the shop window, a job usually performed by the manager, a completely hairless red-faced man with a wide girth and a special interest in pork pies and his young female assistant, who I had seen in the past loitering near the Lion and Unicorn with Joey Dewsbury, a warrior to be avoided. He seemed to be lulled into a false sense of confidence in my ability to perform tasks of a higher level of responsibility than merely mopping up, although I had not yet served a customer.

> *"Eeyar Georgie son, 'ere's a job for yer. Yer 've seen*
> *me do it, 'ave a go yerself. "*

He gave me a piece of paper with the offers written on it and a pint-sized pot of whitewash with a small paintbrush, pointing me to a section of the window inside the shop where he wanted his prices displayed. Then he went over to his bacon slicer and busied himself slicing off some rashers. As he did this I noticed him winking at his deputy who was in charge of the bread and buns, a buxom girl with a beehive hairdo who wore a black bra under her white nylon overall, accentuating her attributes, with a pair of hoops dangling from her ear lobes. Now came a challenge. I had seen him do it, and I knew what was required. My handwriting did leave a lot to be desired when the job was finished and streams of whitewash dribbled down the window. Nonetheless, he seemed to be satisfied with my work and nodded his approval, grinning over his bacon slicer. The beehive was tittering.

> *"Well done, son. Dat'll make 'em stop and 'ave a look.*
> *Now go and put da kettle on and 'ave a brew. A good*
> *job well done."*

I went into the back room to put the kettle on and instantly heard the titter from the beehive develop into a high-pitched cackle and the manager telling her to be quiet. When I returned from my break, fully sated from three of Scott's fine crusty rolls and a jam doughnut, I noticed a group of old ladies outside the shop pointing at my painted sign, cackling to one another. The jaunty delivery man, of a similar stature and gait to Norman Wisdom and who had retrieved the relics of the custard tarts from the South Road calamity, bounced onto the scene with his tray of fresh produce balanced on one hand above his head, paused, and looked in the direction of the gawping group of women. Immediately his pockmarked pasty face creased into a jovial grin.

> *"Eye-eye Jimmy, I see you've caught 'im then. Ripe*
> *one 'ee is, isn't 'ee. Daft little bugger fell down da*
> *trap door in South Road. 'Ee walked backwards down*
> *it. I would have thought 'ee'd 'ave no trouble writing*
> *back to front, seeings he walks backwards. Dey told*
> *me dey used to see 'im walking backwards on 'is way*
> *to school. 'Ee's Michael's brudder."*

The beehive was now bent double screeching with laughter, with a fist over her mouth and the other hand supporting her weight on the counter. She had two rivers of black mascara running down her face, and her beehive hairdo was vibrating. I hadn't realised that I needed to write the details back to front in the window, or they wouldn't be legible from the outside. The pork pie gourmet grinned at me.

> "Dat was a good one 'ey Georgie, dat was a good one was'n it? I didn't know you'd fell down da trap door in South Road though. Dose wimmin der, dey must still be laffin der 'eads off. I hope your Michael doesn't know about it yet, cos I'd love to see 'is face when 'ee finds out."

The day proceeded with the jovial manager grinning at me, and the beehive occasionally breaking into a splutter. However, his joviality was soon to disappear due to an incident involving a delivery bicycle, the groceries contained therein, and my insatiable appetite for a game of football, which was to mark my demise as a figure of fun and remove the garish grin from his sunny tomato-like countenance. It also marked a new chapter in my whistle-stop excursion through the grocery trade.

The following day was a Saturday and I had been selected to play in a five-a-side tournament that morning. I had assumed, wrongly, that I was not working. Seeing that there were only six potential players available and two of them were goalkeepers, the selection procedure was not a prerequisite, save for the arguments over who would play centre forward. It came as something of a blow when I was told that I was supposed to take the delivery bike out and drop off groceries to several customers in the area. This blow was softened slightly when I realised that I could exploit the use of the bike to ride to the playing field and then deliver the groceries afterwards and no-one would be any the wiser. Also, one of the drop-offs was to be the home of Mrs Moran, the mother of celebrated local hero Ronnie Moran, the famous Liverpool full back. So, not only would I be able to ride the delivery bike to the ground, but I might even get a glimpse of Billy Liddell's friend's mother.

The plan worked like clockwork. I loaded up and cycled off in plenty of time for the ten-thirty kick-off. After parking the bike under a tree and getting my boots on, I was soon in the thick of it, playing a blinder with only the occasional toe-ender. I even scored a goal. I remember it well. It was a toe-ender that went wrong but ended up right. The sunshine then turned to showers. On returning to my bike, I found it lying in a large puddle on its side – sans groceries and minus its bell and pump.

On my cautious return to the shop, the jolly red face had turned ashen. The grin was replaced by a threatening glower.

"Where 'av you been, you little bugger? I've 'ad three customers in 'ere raising da bloody roof! Mrs Moran says we can stuff it, she's going to da Maypole instead from now on."

I tried to explain the difficulty I had experienced as a result of my double-booking, but he just wouldn't pay attention. The clincher came when I tried tactfully to inform him of the robbery of the groceries, the bell and the pump.

"Bugger off home now, and when you come back Monday morning, you can 'av yer cards."

I didn't quite know what he meant by this, but rather than ask him I sidled off out of the door, leaving the bike up against the window, a place I had been told never to leave it, but the excitement of the moment left me somewhat confused.

Bright and early on the Monday morning I returned to the shop, still unaware of what was meant by giving me my cards. However, the conundrum was left unsolved, because the manager was standing at the door his face devoid of his usual grin, which was replaced by a sullen frown.

"Don't think yer cummin in 'ere, 'cos yer not. You are a friggin' liability, dat's what you are. Dey nearly gave me me cards, let alone yew. I don't know why

*der doin' it, but dey are keepin' you on. Just 'cos
Scott's sunshine bread shines out of yer brother's arse,
dey think yew must be worth another try. Get yer
backside down to da Bridge Road branch now, and
don't stop off for a kick around on da way, ya daft
bugger. And stay away from my shop!"*

*

The Bridge Road branch was not far from the dairy where my
previous employer had misunderstood my genuine resolve to deliver
his milk to the correct doorsteps on time, in the correct quantity,
and without creating too much clatter. I was, therefore, just a little
concerned that our paths might cross and my history relating to
the dairy industry, especially the scandalous and totally unfounded
slander regarding the six bottles of orange juice, would filter through
to the grocery trade. However, I soon overcame this anxiety when
I was welcomed as a sort of celebrity by the two assistants, one an
Irish boy who I vaguely recognised, and the other a very bouncy girl
with a round cheery face. My reputation for blunders had already
been broadcast throughout the area by the Norman Wisdom clone,
and these two assistants were eager to see what would happen next.
They would not have too long to wait.

This area was at the beginning of the more refined part of
Waterloo bordering Blundellsands, in whose large and sumptuous
houses some of the more affluent patricians of Liverpool society
lived, many of the residents being local minor dignitaries and
celebrities who stood, as far as possible, aloof from their close fellow
citizens and to some extent from one another. Tranquil and grand it
may have been, but sterility seeped from the bricks and mortar which
held it together – the very bricks and mortar bought by slave traders
from the enormous profits of their transactions in human misery. The
occasional relatively successful shopkeeper, upwardly mobile slum
landlord, or prosperous fence undiscovered by the constabulary, was
said to blend with the local society of gin and jags without concern
for, or suspicion of, their mendacity.

Also camouflaged from view, although not next to one another,
were a convent and an unmarried mothers' home, wherein Brides of

Christ would pour out their spleen over the wretched shorn heads of these victims of a society which was firm in the concept that love outside marriage could never be accepted; indeed, the children of these unions were even deprived of the love of their mothers. I used to deliver milk to the unmarried mothers' home not knowing what it was at the time, sometimes seeing a sad face through a window. I would occasionally catch a glimpse of the pious pinch-faced witches with their heads shielded by big headdresses with what appeared to be the wings of swans floating on the top of them – no doubt kept pristine and starched by their captives – with a mass of rosary beads swinging over their dry bosoms. Once when I was about six years old, I discovered in the road a chain of rosary beads with large ebony cross attached and took it home as a present for my mother, unknowingly provoking a major panic attack created by the distress and horror of having it in my possession. It was hastily wrapped in newspaper and put in the dustbin and I was made to swear that I had never seen it. Unfortunately, this promise was void because, unbeknown to my mother, Alfie Littlehales had tried it on and offered me a piece of liquorice in exchange for it, which I had gallantly refused in the certain knowledge that it would look far better around the neck of my mother than dangling from his scrawny shoulders, although the offer was refused primarily because of my dislike of liquorice.

The manager of the Bridge Road branch was in keeping with the area. He was a sinewy Scotsman with an eye for exactitude, as could be deduced from the flawless display of products, the shiny floor, his shiny razor-sharp creased trousers, his shiny shoes, the sheen of which blended with the floor, and his black shiny hair parted in the middle with not a strand out of place. In the top pocket of his pristine white coat were inserted a row of coloured ballpoint pens. No pencil behind the ear for him. And he wore sock suspenders, a device attached to the legs above the calf, with the elasticated straps dangling from them intended to be fastened to socks, to aid them in an attempt to defy the force of gravity.

"Dinna ya think that I'll tak any nonsense fra yoo,
sonny. Ya here ta work an' work ya shall. We dinna

tak noo slackers here. If ya wanna play fitba' ya canna no' do it in the firrms time. Noo get properly dressed an' report to Mr Reilly, and he'll show ya what ya job's goin' ta be. Remember, noo nonsense, or it's ya cards ye'll be gettin'."

Cards again. What they meant by this I had no idea. Patrick Reilly grinned over at me and nodded in the direction of his domain, conveniently close to the bacon slicer. He had a quiff and a DA (duck's arse) combed into the back of his jet-black greased hair. Beneath his white overall he wore light blue drainpipe trousers and black thick crepe-soled suede shoes with shiny buckles on them. He manifested a slight squint which gave him a quizzical air. He was a Ted.

"Are yew still kicking dem over da bar den Georgie?"

The penny dropped. He once played football for St Edmund's Catholic school, and I had played against them alongside gangly Nobby Thomas and the diminutive Biddy Marsh, a label which was acquired because of his small stature, the periodic infestation which arose in his head and the subsequent cranium-soaking in liquid paraffin received by anyone who had been in close contact with him. This rather extreme treatment would have been held against him, save for the fact that he could cross a ball into a goalmouth with pinpoint accuracy and was blessed with a sunny countenance. Fatty Cowan, who was unable to kick a football in a straight line, had a penchant for threatening anyone six inches shorter than himself. He was once invited by me to a physical confrontation at the back of the Odeon in response to his baiting of Biddy Marsh and his infested head. The incident petered out before any blood was spilt. A crowd of interested observers, who had been made aware of the event on the grapevine hours previously and who had gathered in a circle around the combatants, made so much noise that the surrounding neighbourhood was alerted that a fight was in progress. An old lady accompanied by a walking stick appeared on the scene, dispersing the onlookers with it just after I had given Cowan a right jab and he had grabbed me around the throat in an attempt to strangle me.

Reilly had a point. I always managed to kick more over the bar than under it, despite all of Algy's constructive advice.

> *"Yer need ta keep yer 'ead over da ball more, kick it*
> *wid da top of yer foot, and don't lean back. Den yewl*
> *score a bag full."*

I assumed that being placed in the immediate vicinity of the bacon slicer was a form of promotion, but Patrick doubted this.

> *"Old Jock won't let anyone wirk it – it's 'is pride*
> *and joy. He polishes de arse off of it, so he does.*
> *Customers 'av complained dat der bacon smells of*
> *Brasso."*

Even so, I was allowed to serve some customers who had basic requirements. This was a big step up in my involvement with the grocery trade, although matters did not seem so rosy by the end of my first day. The slicing of the corned beef was a case in point. My first effort at surgically carving half a pound of corned beef was returned later in the day by the mother of the little girl who had been sent to buy it.

> *"This looks like it has been sliced by a gibbon ... who*
> *on earth would consider serving this mess up?"*

The question was addressed to Patrick in a cut-glass Liverpool quasi-upper-class accent which was the preserve of some of the Blundellsands pseudo-urbane. He shrugged his shoulders and nodded towards the manager. A woman like this once referred to me as an urchin. Not knowing what an urchin was at the time, I took it as a compliment to me and Albert in respect of our quest to release ants from their prisons under the flagstones using ice-lolly sticks. She happened to be the wife of the manager of the Raven, a pub in South Road. Her son Peter lost his cub cap on a visit to Chester Zoo, where it was inadvertently dropped into the bear pit and he cried all the way home, even through the Mersey Tunnel in the charabanc where it was forbidden to make a noise because the driver could be disturbed and we would all crash and die. I claimed innocence in regard to this misdemeanour, but I was blamed nonetheless, which resulted in another doorstep confrontation for my mother to contend with.

> *"Ees a bit shakey dis mornin'. I tink 'ee might 'a been 'avin a sniff of da barmaid's apron."*
>
> *"Well you can just take it back and slice me some more. I always thought that man was not quite right in the head."*

She looked disdainfully sideways across at the dapper little manager who was vigorously rubbing the marble surface of his counter with a cloth, removing any invisible micro-organisms which might have been present, unaware of the outrageous lie which was being concocted by Patrick Reilly. Patrick skilfully sliced a neat bundle of corned beef for the lady and retrieved the lumps which I had prepared, deftly slipping them under the counter. She was pacified, probably because she noticed that the needle on the scales upon which the meat was weighed pointed nearer to a pound in weight rather than the half-pound that had been previously bought.

> *"Well, I'm pleased to see that the staff here are a lot more professional than the management."*

This remark was addressed piercingly in the direction of the management as she flounced out of the shop, at which point the management abruptly ceased his attack on microbes and jumped to attention, puzzled and somewhat distraught by this verbal attack from a customer of long standing and refinement. His wits returned only after she had left the premises.

> *"I dinna ken what's been goin' on here, but I wouldnae be far off the mark tae think that you had somethin'*

tae doo with this little ootburst of customer discontent,
Mr Reilly. Just you be watchin' yersel' laddie, or its
yer cards ye'll be gettin'."

The Irish boy shrugged his shoulders, presenting an expression
of feigned innocence and wide-eyed bewilderment.

The repatriated slabs of corned beef were turned into the innards
of several crusty rolls and consumed when the management went
to the bank to deposit the takings. The round-faced girl became a
willing party to this. I felt a little guilty about it all, but my new-found
friend put my mind at ease somewhat with a shaky, but convincing
argument in justification.

"Sure, it would only 'ave gone in da bin, and if Jock
'ad found out its yer cards you'd 'ave been gettin',
an' no mistake about dat. I'll mention it when I go to
confession."

The cards yet again. Anyway, I lumbered on under the tutelage
of my genial colleague, albeit a supporter of Everton FC but
nonetheless one like me who felt football was an important, if not
the most important, component in the blending of life as we knew
it. Under his instruction I became an expert corned beef slicer and
quite well-informed in the variety and constituents of the various
loaves and confectionery on sale, as well as an unofficial sampler
of the merchandise. Things seemed to be blossoming in the bakery
business, but the management was lulled into a false sense of
security as I grew ever more confident of my position in the firm.
Everything descends into a state of disorder eventually – that is the
nature of things, although for me the descent is usually rapid and
unexpected, as was the case with the Christmas display. The shock
waves still reverberate.

On a day during the first week of December I arrived to find
the shop window festooned in tinsel, with a large pyramid of jars
of mincemeat resting on a glass shelf with a row of Scott's finest
Christmas Yule Logs laid out beneath them in a straight line like

guardsmen on parade, and on the floor of the display was a crate of eggs cushioned in straw and tinsel. This remarkable spectacle could only have been the work of one man – the resolute and shiny manager. When I entered the shop he was beaming. The dour countenance was replaced by a self-satisfied smile, which on another face could be wrongly interpreted as a lecher's leer. His normally perfectly vertical shiny tie was askew, his normally perfectly groomed hair was uncombed, and his normally shiny shoes were scuffed.

> *"And what d'ye thinks of yon display young man?*
> *Och I've been at it since the wee sma oors, but it was*
> *worth it, dinna ya ken?"*

I nodded my approval, but inwardly recalled my own expertise at building walls from rubble, which I thought was much more creative than a load of jars piled on top of one another.

> *"Well just you learn from this example, sonny, if*
> *ye want t'be in the grocery trade, ye've got to use*
> *the brain the good lord has given ye to attract the*
> *customers. Apply yersel an' ye'll gae a lang way.*
> *Fitba'll get ye nowhere in this world. Noo let's roll*
> *our sleevies up and start the day."*

As the day wore on, a clutch of regular customers came into the shop for their bread and cakes, tinned salmon and slices of bacon. A few passers-by glanced fleetingly at the bold Christmas display in the window. Just before lunch, however, a punter had been hooked. Bullet-proof stockings, tweed suit, felt hat with a pheasant's feather in it, and a face that would stop a clock, according to Patrick. What followed is ingrained in my mind – I still have flashbacks. She marched in on her sturdy tightly laced brown brogue shoes with the air of a brigadier and confronted me.

> *"I would like two jars of your mincemeat please, and a*
> *tin of your sockeye salmon."*

And then I did it. During my short career in the grocery trade I admit to a few minor misfortunes, but this one was an out-and-out calamity. The manager smiled and nodded to me with his eyebrows raised in a confirmatory gesture signifying he was spot-on in his previous conversation with me. The smile then vanished and transformed into an expression of shocked anguish when I walked over to his display and removed two jars of mincemeat from the side of his magnificent pyramid. The resultant collapse of it into the Yule logs was disaster enough, but the ultimate catastrophe arose not because most of the mincemeat and the Yule logs fell into the crate of eggs, but because the jars of mincemeat had cracked the shop window on the way down. This re-vamped display created a great deal more outside interest than had been the case earlier in the day when it had been regulated by methodical and painstaking design. Patrick and the round-faced girl were ecstatic.

The outcome of this unintended act of sabotage is a blur. All I can remember is a very angry Scotsman.

> *"On yer way, sonny, on yer way the noo! Dinna ye bother clearing up, ye'll noo doubt bring tha bloody shop doon if ye try. I'll have yer carrds awaitin' ye in the mornin'. A bloody disaster, that's wha' it is, a bloody tragedy."*

More cards. This time, I thought, I shall get to know what they are. And yet, it didn't happen. It would seem that for Thomas Scott, in some circumstances, the quality of mercy was not strained and the cards, once more, were not put on the table.

I arrived next morning subdued and sheepish, having noticed the sticking plaster over the six-inch crack in the glass and the non-existent display with tinsel hanging forlornly in the gap where the provisions had been so meticulously exhibited. As I entered, Patrick walked over to me with an expression of reverence bordering on admiration. I looked past him in the direction of the bacon slicer, expecting to see the dark countenance of the manager glowering at me with good reason, but he was nowhere to be seen.

102

*"Hey der Georgie boy! Sure dat was a fine
performance you gave us all yesterday. Auld Jock was
boilin' over, so he was."*

"Where is he?"

*"He was told to take da day off, so he was. Dey didn't
want a burst blood vessel makin' more of a mess. Dey
told him his display was a danger to da public, so
you are in da clear, so you are. Dey has made me da
manager for da day so you've done me a big favour,
so you have.*

He was beaming with pride at his temporary promotion,
preening his slick DA with a small comb. The round-faced girl was
gazing across at him with uninhibited approbation, spellbound by
his sudden elevation to the management of her for the day. He cast
a sideways glance over to her, and then turned his asymmetrical
eyes back to me and winked.

*"Just nip into da back Judy, and make Georgie and me
a brew. Den you can look after da shop while we talk
business."*

'Talking business' entailed a conversation about Davey
Hickson's inconceivable recent traitorous transfer from Everton
to Liverpool FC, the inexplicable concepts relating to the off-side
rule, the knockers on Judy, and the fact that I was to continue my
stampede through the branches of the home of good bread with yet
a further relocation to the Crown Buildings shop. So after a final
cupcake we said our goodbyes, and the next morning I hopped on
a bus to my new workplace.

*

The Crown Buildings shop was one of the jewels set in the crown of
the empire of dough presided over by Thomas Scott, being situated in
an area which was busy, and yet emitted a flavour closely associated
with village life of a time gone by. Many of the customers were

residents of the nearby ancient recusant village of Little Crosby, surrounded by the rich soil of the area in which only three or four years previously I had been pea and potato picking for pennies and cavorting in the nearby Sniggery Woods with a bamboo bow and arrows.

My next manager seemed to be a cut above all the others I had met on my swift journey through the establishment. He had what was – I became aware of later in life – a laconic attitude to his position and was epigrammatic but nevertheless courteous in his short but to-the-point conversations with everyone. He had an air of Gotch about him, minus the baggy trousers and Hitleresque hairstyle. He wore wire-rimmed spectacles perched on the end of his nose, and looked imperiously over them at me as I sauntered into the shop spot on time.

> *"Good morning. I see you are here on time. Good start.*
> *Clean the front and pull the sunblind down."*

And that was it. No lecture, no indication that he had reason to believe I was a destructive liability. No pens in top pocket. A stern exterior but indifferent to lesser beings, indicating by his language and demeanour that as long as I left him alone, he would leave me alone.

His assistant was another Irishman, smaller and older than Patrick and with an air of gentle resignation in his manner. He smiled a pleasant greeting to me as he entered, and when he nodded a lock of hair fell down his forehead, giving him foppish appearance. He spoke with a soft Dublin burr complimenting his benign appearance.

> *"Well hallo Georgie boy, sure it is a pleasure to meet*
> *you. Your reputation goes before you, so it does. I*
> *saw young Pat last night, and he says you have the*
> *makings of a fine footballer if you can just keep your*
> *head over the ball. The shop window incident is the*
> *talk of the town. Come on in now and we'll get to*
> *show you what to do. I've been given my instructions*

*to stick to you like a limpet. Sure, I'll be happy for
some pleasant company."*

He turned his head slightly, casting a glance in the direction of
a female assistant who was glowering at him across the floor. She
was a buxom lady with bleached hair, whose white coat strained
to contain her upper attributes, bursting at the buttons. A splash of
scarlet camouflaged the outline of her lips and she was perilously
balanced on a pair of red high-heeled shoes. She winked at me.

*"You just be careful, Georgie boy, or she'll have her
wicked way with you. The van man is petrified of her,
so he is."*

And true enough, when the Norman Wisdom clone appeared
with the day's confectionery balanced on his palm above his head,
his demeanour was subdued and watchful. The jaunty gait had
been substituted by a more moderate approach as he sidled into the
shop without his manic grin and devoid of his wounding repartee.
He edged into the stock room, avoiding eye contact with anyone.
Because he'd avoided eye contact, he was unaware that the high
heels had clattered their way into the same room seconds before he
entered the shop. The discussion which spilled out into the shop
was priceless.

*"Now Rosie, I've told yer before, don't do dat! I'll
drop da bleedin' tray. What'll your Billy say if he
finds out? 'Ees a big bugger is your Billy, and yer
know 'ees already warned me, and I wasn't even doin'
nowt."*

*"Well den, if 'ee thinks yer doin' sumthin', yer might as
well do it den. Eeyar, take a look at dose – dey'll get
yer goin' won't dey?"*

There was a sound of scuffling and then a scarlet-faced van man
shot out of the room, dropped the paperwork on the counter and
made a bee-line for the pavement.

*"I'm not coming back 'ere until she goes! She's a
bloody nymphomaniac, dat's what she is. Someone
else can collect the empty trays."*

The enigmatic expression on the face of the manager remained
intact as he peered over his spectacles as a tottering apparition
emerged from the back room, tossing her peroxide curls and
buttoning up her white coat with difficulty. The outline of her scarlet
mouth seemed to have extended to her ears.

*"Might I remind you that this is a bread shop and not
a knocking shop? Also, your shoes are not in keeping
with the environment in which we operate."*

She shrugged, he said no more. He was adept at mincing beef,
but never his words.

A week passed and nothing untoward happened as my time in
the grocery trade was drawing to a close. Excitement and trepidation
jostled in my head as the time for my enlistment drew closer. Then,
just two weeks before I was due to hand in my notice, the culmination
of all my mishaps seemed to pale into insignificance. I was called
to the bacon slicer – for some reason all the managers seemed to
base themselves at the bacon slicer.

"Do you think you can do something responsible?"

It was a rhetorical question.

"Take this to the bank and don't be too long."

This was, for me, the ultimate accolade. I was entrusted with the
week's takings to deposit in the bank. There were three banks within
walking distance, and I naturally went to the nearest. It was the first
bank I had ever been in and I was enthralled by the significance of
the surroundings. My parents didn't have bank accounts. Sombre

dark oak and a respectful silence, only occasionally broken by the clacking of shoes across the polished stone floor. There was quite a long queue, but I was happy standing there soaking up the atmosphere and watching the various business proprietors depositing hundreds of pounds.

My turn came after nearly half an hour. I strolled up to the counter with an air of self-significance, but when I passed the canvas bag of money and the paying-in book over, my confidence ebbed as the lady cashier smiled at me in a disdainful manner. I was in the wrong bank! Nearly half an hour waiting in the wrong bank.

The outcome of this blunder was a hurried dash to the correct bank some distance away, and a further fifteen-minute wait. When I eventually arrived at the front of the queue, I was taken by surprise when this lady behind the counter knew who I was and where I had come from.

> *"We've had a phone call from Scott's, dear. They were asking where you are. We told them you hadn't been in. I think they are a bit worried about you."*

'Worried' was a glorious understatement. Not only was the high-heeled harpy tottering around Crown Buildings on the lookout for me, but the police had been called on the off-chance that I could have done a runner with the takings. My explanation to the manager came as some sort of respite for him, and he contacted the police again to let them know the matter had been resolved.

This time the cards were definitely on the table. After sanity had been restored, I was once more called over to the bacon slicer. He looked over his wire rims dolefully and addressed me in a resigned fashion.

> *"This ...is ... it. We cannot take any more. You will have to go."*

Precise and to the point.

"It doesn't matter, 'cos I'm leaving anyway. I'm joining the army."

A stunned silence ensued. And then a golden line was articulated which I took as a splendid compliment, and which has lived with me ever since.

"Oh, really? Well, all I can say is that Thomas Scott's loss is Russia's gain."

And so ended, much to my brother's relief, my short but interesting career in buns and bacon, and I didn't ever get to find out what my cards were.

10

THE LEAVING OF LIVERPOOL

Prior to my journey into the unknown military satellite of Bordon in Hampshire, near the massive garrison town of Aldershot, I had what was supposed to be my interview, accompanied by my father, at the London Road recruiting office in Liverpool. I played no part in it. I was still only fourteen, and parental consent was required, which my father was only too happy to agree to after carefully questioning the red-faced, round-bellied, much-decorated recruiting sergeant about whether or not "there is any of that funny business going on". There seemed to be a dark side to his questioning which hung in the air for a few moments. Baden-Powell's reference to 'beastliness' sprang to mind. The recruiting sergeant's face grew a shade redder and his bull neck seemed on the verge of detonation. He spread his stubby fingers wide across a groaning ancient wooden desk as he stood up and gazed across the dank grey room which was dominated by a large framed print of the Annigoni painting of the Queen, and gave my father a glare of hurt indignation. A china mug half-full of stagnating tea wobbled precariously and the overladen ash-tray next to it quivered menacingly.

> *"If you are thinking what I think you are thinking sir, you should be ashamed of yourself. This man's army is a MAN's army and we don't have any accommodation for people like that in our barrack rooms."*

My father seemed satisfied by his indignant reply and offered the sergeant a Woodbine. He happily accepted the offer and they then settled down for a smoke and to an in-depth discussion about the war and the way we sorted the Germans out, my father knowledgeable as ever, no doubt because of his familiarity with *The Listener* stored away in the attic. And that was my interview. On the way home I was slightly puzzled by the manner in which this interview had proceeded and whether or not I was acceptable to the military.

> *"Dad, what did you mean when you talked about funny business?"*
>
> *"Never you mind. There isn't any anyway, so you don't need to bother about it. All you need to do is pass your entrance test and the medical. And don't think because you are leaving you don't have to send any money home."*

That oft-repeated comment still rankles within me.

A couple of weeks later I returned to London Road, this time alone, and was shown into a room with desks where about twenty men sat in various states of dishevelment. In strutted a sleeker version of the recruiting sergeant who had interviewed my father.

> *"Right, you men. No time to mess about. No use lying because we have ways and means of finding out. Hands up those who've been to prison."*

About half of them raised their hands.

> *"Sorry lads, we cannot help you today. If you leave a list of your convictions and sentences before you go we may be able to get back in touch with some of you. We need hard men, but we don't want any villains."*

The next question had a stunning reply, because all but three of the remainder of the group were told there was no place for them in the modern army. They were illiterate. This was the first time in my life I found myself at the top of the class. I then proceeded to pass my pre-entrance tests (no mention of a twelve times table or fractions) to indicate to someone in authority that I could spell my name and write a short note on why I wanted to be a soldier. I cannot remember exactly what I wrote, but I do know I mentioned my proficiency as a boy scout and mentioned some of the badges I had acquired including camper, cook, messenger, first aider and fire-fighter. I also exaggerated my skills as a footballer as I always have, even to this day. It's easy to beat a seven-year-old to a tackle at sixty and boast about your skill with impunity.

I was then directed to a room with cubicles, to be medically investigated to ensure that I was free from venereal disease, head lice, had no perceptible mental deficiency, and was physically fit to undertake the rigours of army life. I joined a line of more adult recruits who seemed to tower over me, some of whom looked at me suspiciously, puzzled by both my size and apparent age. My balls were squeezed by an old man in a white coat; he investigated my head for nits and my still-sprouting pubic hair for crabs, whispered something behind my back to check my hearing, did some prodding and poking at my abdomen and to my horror inspected my anus. Dr Novak would have shredded him. At the time I had only that year recovered from another bout of pneumonia, weighed in at eight stone and had a thirty-two inch chest. It was noted that I was a Caucasian. I found this to be a bit of a mystery, because I was under the impression that I was a Liverpudlian. When I later eventually arrived at the drill square for an initiation into the skills of turning right and left, swinging the arms and digging the heels in, my Liverpudlian antecedence was reinstated in no uncertain manner, by the NCO in charge of turning a herd of juvenile oddities and miscreants into a well-oiled military machine.

> "Now 'ear me, and 'ear me well, you boys. This intake
> 'as among you a Scouser. Two things I 'ave to say
> to you. One, keep your money in your pockets. Two,
> keep your lockers locked at all times. We don't trust
> no Scousers 'ere, they're worse than the Welsh."

My anguished mother took me to Liverpool's Lime Street station to say goodbye and ensure I boarded the correct train. In common with most adolescent boys, I was embarrassed and angry at her maternal solicitude, especially when she attempted to give me a hug and then help lever me into the innards of the giant hissing iron horse, which was impatiently gasping and spluttering out corkscrews of steam and smuts, eager to convey me on a journey into the unknown. We were never a tactile family – working-class Victorian reserve had seen to that many years before I was born. After all, I was off to be a soldier and this sort of display of affection was just not on. The word 'love' was never mentioned in our house.

As I settled down alone into my seat in the austerely cushioned, wooden-framed and mirrored compartment, I felt perhaps for the first time, how small and insubstantial I was in the face of all that might follow. As I crossed for the first time over the huge cantilever railway bridge spanning the Mersey, my bravado faded into a haze of apprehension that I couldn't express. The feeling sometimes returns even now – "who am I, what am I doing?" From that day the philosophic meanderings of Popeye – *I am what I am, and that's all that I am* – began to take on more resonant connotations; much later in life Plato was waiting in a second-hand bookshop somewhere to inform me in greater depth. I was soon to learn that the die is cast. Regardless of any changes we attempt, and sometimes succeed at, part of us remains always the same; we are what we were born into. I am still the kid from the outskirts of Liverpool who came out sideways and who bestrode the fault-line, neither poverty-stricken, nor respectable but in the middle, kicking toe-enders.

To come from being poor to being comfortable is not a rung on the ladder. It may seem so to some from both ends of the spectrum, but a pedigree is still as much of a dog as a mongrel. I take solace in the approach of the stoic warrior emperor Marcus Aurelius – we are as old as the day, no older and no younger. We cannot have the past, and we cannot have the future. We can only have what is. We may change our accents, our dress, our politics and our social mores, and perhaps even in some cases despise our antecedence, all to no or little avail. Kipling could never have been more wrong when he alleged – in condescending doggerel – that

> *The Colonel's lady an' Judy O'Grady*
> *Are sisters under their skins!*

No they are not, nor will they ever be. They may both be human, but close relatives? For all his military ramblings, Kipling – like my father – knew everything but never served a day.

*

Some seven hours later my train terminated at Euston Station with a jolt, and I descended hesitantly onto a platform awash with a sea of people in a cloud of smutty steam and replete with a stomach crammed with sandwiches and fruitcake. When I walked into the main concourse I had the feeling that I was lost and would stay lost for ever in the seething, steaming mass of people criss-crossing my own winding path. My instructions were to take the underground to Waterloo, a destination which seemed all the more apposite when I noticed an old man selling newspapers and thought of benign bent old Jack. And then I had my first involvement with a chirpy old cockney.

> *"Excuse me, sir – how do I get the underground to Waterloo?"*
> *"D'ya wanna buy a pyper mate?"*
> *"No thank you."*
> *"Well fack orf then."*

So I facked off, bemused and disturbed by my very first encounter with someone who spoke like Tommy Trinder and showed scant regard for children in difficulties, because in spite of my bravado, I was still a child. Liverpool, this was not. I was concerned about approaching anyone else for fear of an even worse encounter, but then I noticed in the middle of the mayhem a cubicle offering information with two burly military policemen standing outside. I approached with caution, and as I did so one of them beckoned me over with the crook of his index finger. I was now in the Army, and for all its future faults and despicable contradictions, I became aware that no matter how awful things might get, there would always be someone to ease the path.

"Where are you going son?"

"I am trying to find the underground to Waterloo, sir."

*"Don't call me sir, you call me corporal. Only officers
are called sir. Are you National Service? You look too
young."*

"No sir, I mean corporal, I'm a Junior Leader."

*"Oh, another Junior Bleeder eh? Well sonny, I don't
know why you did it, but you're in the Army now –
there's no going back. What mob are you joining?*

"The RASC, corporal."

"Run Away Someone's Coming, eh?"

The joke was lost on me. He shook his head and grinned at me,
and then patted me on the shoulder, and I grew two metaphoric feet
in stature. Here was I, a soldier in London, being assisted to my unit
by a big jovial military policeman. Things were looking rosy. And
then he gave me a piece of advice and a piece of chocolate.

*"No matter what happens, don't ever let them know
you are frightened of them, and never, ever, volunteer
for anything."*

I was not sure who he was talking about, but in his next breath
he explained.

*"The buggers who train you will try to scare you, but
believe me sonny, they are all piss and wind. I'm
doing my National Service with three weeks to go,
and then I'm on my way home."*

His advice turned out to be worthy, and had I not been given
it so early, I might not have developed my otward appearance of
indifference to the verbal contempt which was to be meted out by
some of the adult soldiers in charge of our group of youthful misfits,
Barnardo's boys, borstal boys and boy scouts. Some of them would

crumble and crack within a few weeks, discharged as unsuitable for military service at the age of fifteen, cowed into submission, mentally scarred and with nowhere to go – not even the fault line. Most, like me, would be fortunate in our own self-awareness, not to be duped into believing the contemptuous picture of us painted by a bully with halitosis bawling in our faces from close quarters and turning purple in the process.

My first ever comrade-in-arms walked with me to the entrance to the underground station and pointed me in the direction I should follow, and minutes later I was sitting in the bowels of a rattling giant worm threading its way through a seemingly dark and endless tunnel, flashing and grumbling over the track. The blank faces avoiding eye contact with one another were all unaware that, without the building of the Liverpool Overhead Railway, the electric motors under our feet might never have been considered fit for the London underground system. I felt a tang of smug self-aggrandisement.

My arrival at another Waterloo station, far from that of my still smouldering childhood, was overseen and dominated by an enormous four-faced clock hanging from the roof of the immense concourse, and this time I was able unassisted to find my way to the platform from which a train bound for Liss in Hampshire was waiting to carry me still further into the unknown. Trepidation began to fill the vacuum in my mind, which had suspended reality since stepping onto the platform at Euston station. The unease I sensed was soon to be justified an hour or so down the line, when the train jerked and juddered to a halt at Liss in a windswept downpour, enveloped in darkness. As it trundled off I was left desolate on a platform, waterlogged, shivering and apprehensive as to my fate. The instructions were to go to the station waiting room where transport was arranged to collect me and deliver me to St Lucia Barracks in Bordon. I had by now been travelling for ten hours and wanted to go home. I had eaten all my sandwiches within an hour of leaving Liverpool and hunger was closing in.

Through the murk I could see a hazy yellow light emanating from the outline of a solitary building, and made my way towards what turned out to be the waiting room. Through the haze I could see that there were people inside and this gave me confidence, although it was soon diminished when I opened the door and was confronted by a Dickensian scene of a steaming cluster of wet unkempt boys, all waiting for transport to what was to turn out to be an earthly equivalent of perdition; a place where normal adolescence would be abolished, and the ways of the outside world would be suspended and upended by a big man with a straight back, bulging eyes, a very loud voice, and a stick to measure his pace. The absurdity of what I had done struck me instantly. I was tired, wet, hungry, disoriented and in the army. This was just the beginning of a night of intense trauma. I was now at the mercy of the military machine. I had signed my life away for twelve years on a whim at the age of fourteen via an advertisement I saw in a comic at the age of thirteen, secure in the belief that many of Baden-Powell's boy scouts were warriors in the making, and I was one of them.

After stilted and subdued introductions, the alpha male in the little party – stubby bitten nails, nicotine stained fingers, slicked back black greasy hair, pustules and no front teeth – addressed us.

"This ain't no good is it? If they don't come soon I'm gonna bugger off home."

The raspy Mancunian quack echoed around the dank room. Nobody else spoke. One of them was trying to hide tears that were being forced out of the corners of his eyes. They were betrayed by the streaks of grey on his face caused by wiping his eyes with the cuff of a damp sleeve. We were still children, and this boy's face personified our plight. A world of make-believe had suddenly come to an abrupt and stupefying end; it was a baleful and totally unexpected introduction to soldiering which is imprinted on my mind still, after all these years. The images are so stark that it could have been last night.

Incredibly, I met this same boy when he was a man many, many years later after I had lived a different life as far away from the military as I could get, but had taken up work as a tribunal representative for those who claimed a pension for medical conditions and mental problems caused by the services. He was still crying and his poor wife, who loved him dearly, was at her wits' end.

116

He had been bullied mercilessly for several years and eventually discharged from the military. His plight was put down to his own "lack of moral fibre" and now, in his declining years, all the horrors he had experienced at the hands of bullies had returned to haunt him.

A drone became a fractured roar, and a pair of dazzling headlights came bouncing out of the blustering gloom. They morphed into a Land Rover which juddered to a halt just before entering the building through its brick wall. One of the devil's emissaries to Earth burst out of the driving seat and into the road, bawling against the growl of the engine and the rattle of the wind through the trees. The essence of his shrieked announcement was to the effect that we should all get our arses into the back of the Land Rover very quickly. This we all did, the alpha male first in, the weeping boy last, and myself somewhere in the middle, keeping a low profile. The journey to Bordon was fast and daunting, not only for the passengers, but for the maniac who was driving through this deluge. The windscreen wipers were not working, so he was periodically reaching out of his window to try to wipe the windscreen clear with a pair of waterlogged old underpants. Visibility was down to inches. After about ten minutes, which seemed more like ten hours, the vehicle unexpectedly lurched through an uplifted barrier guarded by a spotty First World War uniformed child holding a pick-axe handle. It was very nearly removed from his hand by the roaring Land Rover, intent on entering the guardroom via yet another brick wall. This boy was soon to become known to me as the RSM's 'favourite soldier'. He was four feet ten inches tall and as such, when performing rifle drill with fixed bayonets, was a fearsome and dangerous person to be close to because he was so short. It was hard for him to manoeuvre the rifle without stabbing the pointed end into the eye of a neighbour. In addition, his 1914-18 cap was a size too large for him and was secured only by his protruding ears, affording him extremely limited vision.

The interior of the guardroom resembled the waiting room, apart from the warmth, shiny floor, sparkling brass handles and a couple of cells with iron barred gates. A large mongrel was sitting dejectedly in the corner of one of them. It turned out that the dog was under arrest and living on reduced rations of bread and water: it had been charged with conduct prejudicial to good order and military discipline in that it had urinated on the guardroom wall. It was also charged with gross indecency, a charge that would be dropped because such a serious crime would necessitate the institution of a court martial.

This was my first experience of the absurdities of military discipline and this experience was attained within minutes of the twelve years' service which lay ahead. It was indicative of much, but not all, of what was to follow. Much later I was to meet a man called Paul Berry, a man who had suffered the same fate as the dog, although he was prosecuted rather than jailed for his misdemeanour. He was the first person in my life to give me a sense of self-worth. He was on the same plane as Billy Liddell, but the chalk of his life and achievements and the cheese of Billy's could never blend, although they were derived from the same earthly constituent – humility.

After some cursory questioning and fractious comment bordering on malice by the guard commander, a soldier with a basin-cut not dissimilar to that of Moe from the Three Stooges with a demeanour to match, directed us through the rain to a hut from which we were to collect basic requirements. These materialised into a mattress, three blankets, two pillows, a pair of sheets, a set of denim work clothes, a pair of boots, a china mug with knife fork and spoon, a webbing belt and gaiters, a set of pyjamas and a beret. A soldier in the stores, referred to by our guide as Fat Henry, produced the equipment and proceeded to load us up and then pointed us through the downpour to a barrack block about fifty yards away. With our mattresses balanced over our heads, we staggered over to it and up the concrete steps like a procession of shield bugs in a hurricane and entered a scene from a *Carry On* film. I recognised it straight away: it was a bog-standard 1950s Ealing Studios barrack room.

There was a reception party of quasi-troglodytes waiting to introduce themselves to the newcomers. One was leaping up and down on the bare bedsprings of what was to be my bed, whooping. He was tall, lank, gormless and threatening. Another three boys were huddled around the stove in the middle of the stale-smelling gloomy room, one poking the ashes and feeding lumps of wood into it from what looked like the remains of a door. Indeed, it *was* a door. The other two were taking turns spitting on the lid of the stove, absorbed by the hissing sound emanating from it. Their bovine activities terminated abruptly when we entered. They encircled us as curious baboons would when about to pick a fight, but not too sure of whether or not it was worth the trouble. The intent was to intimidate rather than offer violence, because they all produced pieces of equipment and clothing which were swapped for our own new kit with a cheery front suggestive of Fagin's jolly band of juvenile robbers.

After the initial introduction to our quarters by these boy warriors, they departed, jabbering, with their loot, dragging the remainder of the door behind them and we were left in silence to consider our troubled circumstances. The fire in the stove faded, the room chilled, and the rain battered the windows. The crying boy was now in full flood, and even the alpha male Mancunian had a layer of pallor tinting his cheeks. This was all Baden-Powell's fault. All because of *Scouting for Boys* and *The Eagle* I had ended up signing on for twelve years in the belief that the military would be the making of me, reinforcing my father's considered opinion that it would straighten my back. I could have made it big in the grocery trade. *Not to worry,* I thought, *perhaps there will be plenty of time to kick balls about.* Happily, this turned out to be true. Fortunately for me, and unbeknown to the military, it did do me much more good than harm – because it gave me a perspective on life and the way it should be survived that would never have entered my head were I destined to spend my working life riding around on a delivery bike. At that moment though, I was very hungry, tired, wet, disoriented and more than a little frightened.

As I was doing my juvenile best to make my bed on a waterlogged foam mattress which by now resembled a sponge, the clatter of boots came striding down the corridor, and in marched a big man with a lantern jaw and a stick. He looked around him incredulously, and for the first time I noticed that the room had no door. It had been ripped off its hinges. His eyes screwed up and he looked at each one of us in turn.

"Well, this is a fine start lads. You've only been here half an hour and a bleedin' door goes missing. Come on now, you boys, what have you done with it?"

119

As he was speaking his eyes fell upon a couple of lumps of wood next to the now inert stove.

"I don't bleedin' believe it! Half an hour, that's all it took and you're in the clink before breakfast."

The thought of not getting any breakfast, when starvation was becoming more and more a certainty as opposed to an imaginary scenario, was the motive for me to speak up and falteringly tell the big man with the stick of our reception committee and the door's demise.

"Get to bed all of you. Lights out in ten minutes. We'll sort this out in the morning."

As if by magic the room seemed to fill up with about fifteen boys all intent on getting into their beds before the lights went out. They had little to say to one another or to us. It transpired that they were new recruits too and had only arrived a few days ago. So far they had spent their free time in the NAAFI to keep warm because their (and our) coal supply had been stolen. So ended my first day as a soldier.

I must have nodded off at some stage, because it seemed as if almost immediately I was awoken by a bugle call; a sound gentle, novel and quixotic. The more brutal and physical awakening arrived almost instantaneously when another man with a stick burst in through the hole in the wall where a door should have been, switched on the lights and proceeded to bang his stick on the dustbin lid he was holding. Then he started banging his stick on the beds of those who were still in them. Mayhem ensued, as a mad scramble to the washhouse developed. Six washbasins with only cold running water and six lavatories for the use of twenty boys: one toilet had no door, probably again the consequence of the lack of coal.

11

REALITY

THE REGIMENTAL PLAN

The clock turned clown and shrieked the dawn
of day, with foolish fingers twisted in a smirk.
It leered at morning's spiky spears of light
that kicked the shades of sleep back to the grave
as conscious thought began to swamp the mind,
recalling things that should be said and done. But
how and why and what and when and if bobbed up
and down inside my bursting brain to make a mock
of life's intended plan, as twisted fate takes hold of
mortal aim.

And then the jagged facts attacked and scratched
the waking head. The floodgates burst as day once
more raked up the cinders of my past. They fanned
again the flame of primal id, defeating time and
rooting in the skull as if today was but tomorrow's
then. They unhinged rod-like reason from the scene,
transforming months to seconds in the mind with
strobes of recall flashing on and off.

And in the still of early morning's calm I saw my
yesterdays again and heard a silent bugle blow the
age-old tune which bolted Kipling's Tommies from
their cots to force them onward in their blood-soaked
schemes; the brawny sons of Blighty's shores and
mills tormenting Fuzzy with their bayonets, pissing
on his idols, ripping out his guts.

I'd heard that tune a hundred times before, and
thought of home in adolescent fear as daybreak
brooded on my crystal boots. They soon would left

and right and smash and crash in time with other
bugles and the drums, behind the peacock peasant
with his stick; the bawling brawling man-beast RSM.
His honour was the regimental plan. His duty was to
shape and make the man.

There is no point in describing in any great depth the privations of life for the next two and a half years. The lot of the national serviceman in the 1950s has been visited time and time again by those who experienced it, and my introduction to army life was no different, other than the fact that I was still a child and that a national serviceman's so-called basic military training lasted a mere three months, whereas a boy soldier's lasted for two-and-a-half years. However, what I can do is speak belatedly for those who didn't survive this outdated and unsavoury practice of the military to meld children into their conception of men suitable for military service, while discarding and humiliating those who didn't or couldn't manage to fit the mould. Bullying was by no means endemic, either by the men in charge or the boys themselves, but it was not uncommon. On the other hand, the concept of bullying is one which can at times go hand-in-glove with what is considered by fools to be 'discipline' and a lot of those fools held the whip hand – literally.

I still vividly remember one of these children, whose situation sets my mind tumbling back in time, glazed in a mist of shame and guilt whenever it is jolted into reverse. He was an ideal victim; an orphan, despised for wanting to be accepted on equal terms as a human being with his tormentors, men and boys alike. He had no-one in the world to turn to. At fifteen years of age he was bereft and alone in the world; downtrodden in a manner that invites brickbats. When leave was granted, he remained in the barracks, for he had no other home to go to. He was always last in the washhouse, last in the cookhouse line, last getting changed for physical training, and last in the weekly cross-country run. Because he was always last to wash, or sometimes never even had the opportunity, he was given a 'regimental scrub'. Because he was always last in the line for food, he was denied much of it, and as for physical training, the abuse was humiliating and degrading. I didn't participate in his breaking, but even at such a tender age I knew I should have had the courage to object to it. The adults with their so-called 'duty of care' who turned a blind eye were as uncivilised as those who perpetrated and actually participated in such cowardly and brutal behaviour.

I believe that the 'regimental scrub' is now proscribed in the British Army, though still subsists clandestinely in some quarters. There are several variants of it, but the one I was aware of was straightforward and simple in its harsh and merciless procedure. He was stripped naked, dumped in a bath of freezing cold water and scrubbed from head to toe with a stiff broom and scouring powder until patches of his skin fragmented. Special attention was given to his genitalia, which had previously been the object of blackening with boot polish. Then his eyebrows were shaved. This further indignity was intended to display to everyone, including inspecting officers, that he had been the subject of a form of discipline meted out to those considered to be unclean.

That experience didn't break him. It was just a matter of course and part of his situation in life's unbending strictures for one such as him. He didn't complain, nor did he cry. He grinned and displayed his shaved inflamed eyebrows as if they were an award for his courage in suffering such humiliation. What did break him a couple of weeks later was being urinated on by a brutal towering hulk of a physical training instructor when the boy was lying on the gym floor unable to perform the number of press-ups required by this menacing man-mountain, who considered it sport to punch boys in the stomach while they were hanging from wall bars, or throw medicine balls at their heads when their backs were turned. He was also an expert at nipple twisting, a brutal, painful torture which caused even greater anxiety than the prospect of being punched in the stomach.

The child absconded, or 'went on the trot', in the then jargon of the army. In fact, because they took so long to find him, he was branded as a deserter at fifteen years of age. The reason his recapture took so long was because he had no-one in the world to go to and so avoided apprehension because of his solitary existence. He was eventually discovered by the police living rough somewhere on a beach on the south coast, physically exhausted and surviving by rummaging through waste bins. He was returned to the unit, immediately put in a cell in the guardroom, charged, sentenced to imprisonment in the military prison at Colchester and soon thereafter discharged dishonourably from the army. This ultimate humiliation ensured that employment in civilian life would be virtually unobtainable because of the disgrace he had allegedly brought upon himself. Where he went afterwards I do not know, but I did think of him often, ashamed of my own spinelessness in not trying to help him. The company sergeant major made himself plain at special muster parade, the morning after the unfortunate child was hauled off to Colchester to serve time alongside the adult criminals. He was not the first, but certainly would not be the last.

> *"Now hear me, and hear me well you boys. You are in the army, and you are in the army until your service expires. If you go on the trot you will be severely punished. If you desert we will hunt you down, punish you, and then WE will desert you. And mark my words; your punishment will be severe. It won't just be bread and water you'll be on, you'll be doubling up and down your own backsides sixteen hours a day before we throw you out into civvie street where you will not be wanted and where you will be despised for the rest of your lives for breaking your promise to Queen and Country. Now I ask you, is it worth it?"*

And with that we marched off for breakfast to the discordant bugles playing out of time with the drums to the tune of the regimental march *Wait for the Wagon*. From that moment, my mind was made up. I would be a soldier in name only, but would never, ever let them know my true feelings. I would play the game, but on my own secret terms. I did, and I survived.

So when the sharp-faced, sharp-uniformed, tin-voiced sergeant screamed down my ear that my parents had been scraped up from the pigeon shit of Trafalgar Square, I continued counting the bricks on the barrack room wall and didn't even feel a flash of contempt. When the porcine Goering-clone, whisky-sodden, cavalry-reject commanding officer prodded me with his swagger stick, turned my bed upside-down and threw my not-polished-enough boots through the window, I didn't even flinch. When I was hauled into the boxing ring to go three rounds with a British amateur boxing champion called Ginger, who was nearly two stones heavier and two years' older than me, instead of covering my head with my hands I took a sideways swipe at him, hitting him on the nose, to wake up a minute later lying sideways with *my* nose broken and bleeding. His nose had been broken so many times it was just a splodge of rubbery flesh more or less in the middle of his grinning face. Incredibly, he re-set my nose on the spot by knocking it back into line. I spent the next two weeks with a face like a panda.

Mistakes like this can sometimes have happy outcomes, and because of this uneven confrontation in the boxing ring – not engineered by him but by a deranged physical training instructor – Ginger became my friend and protector for the next six months, prior to his leaving our community of child-warriors for more adult fields, and Ginger was a person to be reckoned with by both men and boys alike. His grin said it all. It was a 'knowing' grin, an Al Capone grin – not quite manic, not quite threatening, but disturbingly unsettling when flashed. Regardless of his considerable prowess inside the boxing ring, not once did he raise a fist to anyone outside of it. All he needed to do was curl his lips and grin. To my incredulous good fortune he held me in high esteem because I had hit him on his nose. Beware of messing with anyone befriended by Ginger. And so, from that time on, my life was somewhat blessed. I was never locked in my steel locker and had it pushed down the concrete stairs with me inside, none of my kit was stolen, and I never had to scrape the urinals clean with a razor blade.

However, clandestine chores of communal benefit were expected and not objected to. Theft of food from the cookhouse and coal in the winter from the adjoining barracks housing national servicemen were obligatory. Both were always in short supply, especially the coal. I thought that 4 Church Road was cold in the winter, but St Lucia Barracks could well have been situated in the Arctic. The only way to retain a modicum of warmth was to either to steal and burn a door, or to pilfer coal. The latter was by far the more acceptable exercise, because if apprehended violence would occur, but if a door was liberated, the wrath of the sergeant major would not be satisfied until the culprits were locked up in the guardroom. The dichotomy here, though, was that the guardroom had a plentiful supply of coal and the water was not frozen in the taps. I speak from experience.

THE AIM OF EVRY JUNIOR LEADER IS TO BE A FUTURE WARANT OFFICER

This precise but incorrectly spelled banner headline was emblazoned across daily company orders for all junior leaders to see and take heed of, although the subtext was, and no doubt still is, far less apparent; it speaks volumes about the whisky-soaked aging ex-cavalry Officer Commanding hung out to dry, who unrelentingly castigated the children in his care, and his proof-reading ability even when sober. It was subliminally intended to indicate to boy soldiers, regardless of the old saying *'in every soldier's knapsack is a Field Marshall's baton',* that it was nigh impossible, nor was it expected, for any of them to aspire to the officer class; for here is where I was – aged fifteen, poorly educated, and unaware at the time of Wellington's proud assertion that his soldiers were the scum of the earth. Not a grammar school boy among us. Boys from grammar schools didn't become boy soldiers. Some, of course, might become eligible to join the officer class later, if they could show due deference to the system and learn not to drop their aitches and their fathers were not dockers. My brother seemed to be more at ease tapping on his bongos and peering through lensless spectacles when his scholastic contemporaries were singing about Flora's holiday, jolly boating weather, *playing up and playing the game.* These people were not necessarily the intellectual betters of my brother, but socially acceptable betters, of whom some would become officer cadets, world away from my socially and educationally feeble contemporaries, most whom had a functional reading age of only eight years.

Life as a boy soldier in the 1950s has hardly been made the serious stuff of literature, apart from a few dull, self-aggrandising discourses from those who designed and oversaw the system. Some of the crackpots concerned, who likened the system to a public school for working-class youths, actually believed this nonsense.

Many, but not all, of those who trained these young boys in the formative years of their adolescence were indoctrinating them into a set of principles foreign to their young civilian contemporaries, and they were not averse to thrashing them if they felt it necessary to get their message through, although this aspect was not widely publicised in recruitment literature, certainly not in *The Eagle*.

I have a photograph of myself in Buller Platoon, named after the much vaunted General Redvers Buller of Boer War infamy (20,000 heavily armed British and colonial troops against 8,000 farmers), of whom it is said would not allow his soldiers to crawl on the ground in combat because they would dirty their uniforms, or dig foxholes because it might destroy the beauty of the surrounding countryside. After the gruesome and humiliating debacle of Spion Kop he was dismissed from the army, but nonetheless was feted by the public in response to the propaganda of the day. The photograph I have was taken two years into my service, but it speaks volumes regarding the physical condition of many of the little boys who were soon to be designated men. Many of them, but by no means all, looked stunted and malnourished.

Things are different today. My heart is warmed whenever I see a colonel being interviewed on the television and speaking with a regional accent. The Officers' Mess will never be the same! Perhaps earlier in his service as a young subaltern, he may have been confused by a doddering red-nosed brigadier for the mess steward. He certainly wouldn't sneer at my own Liverpool accent in the same way my first platoon commander often did, a second lieutenant with pimples and without a chin, who knew nothing of my background other than that in his eyes it was coarse and of no concern.

I just didn't feel right in the army, but what else could I have done, a fourteen-year-old Boy Scout with his brains in his boots? There was no going back.

12

HOMECOMING

After six months of indoctrination into the world of boy-soldiering, where spitting and polishing, marching around in circles behind dodgy out-of-tune bugles and drums, climbing over rope bridges and being shouted at had become a way of life, I was allowed home for a couple of weeks' leave. I had learned to fire a rifle, a machine gun and a rocket launcher, stick and twist a bayonet into a bag of straw impersonating the enemy, strip and assemble a machine gun, experience the sting of tear gas in a closed concrete room and to swing across a ditch in full marching order with a rifle precariously slung over my round shoulder, just like the advertisement in *The Eagle*. Unlike the boy in the advertisement, I wasn't grinning. I'd had my nipples twisted unmercifully, broken the icicles off taps to wash, slept under my bed to ensure my kit was laid out and ready for inspection the next morning, only to collect it from the road outside in the rain having had it thrown out of the first floor window – including the mattress. However, because of my association with Ginger I was never required to push an open can of boot polish the length of the barrack room floor with my nose in it while naked. Home seemed a distant and almost illusory memory.

When I wasn't polishing brass buttons, I was polishing boots, including the studs and the soles. When I wasn't polishing boots, I was polishing the floor. When I wasn't polishing the floor, I was polishing my belt brasses, my cap badge, my shoulder tags, my gaiter straps, my chin strap. And then there was the scourge of Blanco – the khaki variety. Large pack, small pack, bullet pouches, cross straps, gaiters, bayonet scabbard and belt. All had to be regularly coated in this substance which had the consistency, texture and colour of a loose bowel movement. The smell was not as acrid, but unpleasant nonetheless. A special room was set aside for this activity and hours of communal wallowing were spent there resulting in a condition known at the medical centre as 'Blanco Rash' – raw seeping sores on the hands, particularly between the fingers.

On the first leave home, no civilian clothes were allowed to be worn on departure from these halls of military enlightenment into the strange world of the civilian, a place I used to know where blankets and sheets were never folded every morning into a precise cube, where nipple twisting was regarded as common assault, where doors were not used for firewood and where people slept in their beds and not under them with the contents of their wardrobes laid out neatly on their mattresses. So out I strutted in my WW1 uniform, very shiny boots, a very short haircut and my cap the regulation one inch above the eyebrows, looking like an extra in a silent movie. The world seemed to have changed; I was unaware that it was me who had been changed, but thankfully as it turned out, not irrevocably.

It was impossible to tell my friends of the reality of my new life; boy scouts and boy soldiers are worlds apart and to them I must have looked odd and completely out of place in the budding world of the Liverpool scene in 1960 and I felt it. Here was I, a year younger than them and a soldier, and there were they still at school, some destined to be teachers and others accountants. The army slang which had been imbued in me was incomprehensible to them and it was with difficulty that I refrained from its usage for fear of ridicule. My father beamed with pride at my semi-upright appearance and commented on what a fine pair of shoulders I had gained.

> *"Look at that Jean, he's a walking bloody coat hanger."*

He was lying. My shoulders are still as round as they ever were and I remain to this day envious of those who can hang a bag from theirs without the strap sliding off.

I felt as if I had returned from another planet where nothing but disdain and futile endeavour were paramount. Home was definitely where my heart was, and it was pure delight not to have to sleep under my bed. My friends remained friends for the time-being at least and henceforward I would spend as many weekends as I could hitching lifts on lorries to and from Liverpool, often taking twelve hours or more each way to do it, but confident in my belief that in so doing, I would not become alienated from the world I knew and loved, and that the army would not swamp my mind-set with unpalatable half-truths about who I was and what lay in store for me. I had made up my mind, after the shameful episode regarding the regimental scrubbing of a child, that these people – few though they might be – did not have the right to share my company or determine my place in the world.

13

PAUL BERRY

Having reversed a three-ton truck at considerable speed into a wall due to a mix-up between the clutch and the accelerator, after nearly two months of painstaking and anxious instruction from a man whose hair seemed to grow greyer over the same period, it was decided that my future in the RASC (*Run Away Someone's Coming*) was not to be involved in any way with transport. Prior to this unfortunate occurrence, driving on the road to Portsmouth during one of the rare occasions they took a chance and let me out of the barracks, I'd had the misfortune to remove a broom from a road sweeper's grasp and send it spiralling into the air. The road sweeper was unharmed – in the rear-view mirror I could see his diminishing image jumping up and down and shaking his fist. I remember the benign Motor Transport senior NCO in charge of my instruction being quite vexed by my inability to drive a lumbering Austin K4 lorry, without synchromesh transmission, in a straight line. And in no uncertain terms he told me:

> *"You boy, are a bleedin' mystery. You can strip and assemble a machine gun, hit a target at one hundred yards with a rifle, prime a hand grenade without blowing your bleedin' head off, find your way through a tunnel of shit, climb over a 12 foot wall, you are a qualified marksman (experience gained in the slaughtering of flies with an air rifle saw to that) and yet you cannot point a vehicle in a straight line. You are off the course. God alone knows what would happen if they let you loose on a tank transporter."*

Strangely, he hadn't heard about the Antar tank transporter. Thirty tons of juddering 360 bhp muscular metal. The genial driver of this leviathan should have known better, for he allowed me, a mere stripling, into his driving seat to see how it felt. Over a distance of fifty yards across the barrack square I managed to burn the clutch to such an extent that acrid smoke permeated the cookhouse the same distance away.

What has all this got to do with a man called Paul Berry? This man, unbeknown to him, made me what I am and our fortuitous meeting and subsequent friendship was a direct result of my inability to double declutch.

To keep me away from vehicles, it was decided to move me to an administrative role in the army, especially as it was reported that I was good at reading maps and – incredulously to me – my handwriting was considered more legible than most of my contemporaries. And so I was told to report to a Mr Berry, who was in charge of a small section considered to be the crème de la crème of the intelligentsia in one of the huts masquerading as the Bordon College of Knowledge for future Warrant Officers. There were three of us from a total of over three hundred boys.

Situated alongside this community of mayhem suggestive of the halls of Bedlam, was a mild unobtrusive civilian. He was quietly spoken and slight of frame, and his demeanour seemed to be at odds with the military regarding how a *man* should be. I came to know that all was not as it seemed, as the elderly worldly-wise spinster Miss Shaw had mentioned to me a couple of years prior to my metamorphosis from apple thief to warrior, for this man had a rod of steel for a backbone though few, if any, of my contemporaries ever became aware of it.

Paul Berry was a pacifist and no doubt the whiskey- pickled cavalry officer in charge of us would have had a seizure had he known. Berry was a person who, in my domain, was called a coward, although my contemporaries didn't know he was a pacifist; they just thought he was a mild person of little or no consequence, save that he spoke to them with a civility which surprised them – in sharp contrast to the verbal abuse levelled at them on the barrack square. The irony was that he could never have been the recipient of a white feather because when he joined the army in 1942 as a young man, he worked in bomb disposal, perhaps one of the most courageous tasks of all.

He taught me to write shorthand, and in so doing opened to me a door to the world of literature and the beauty of the English language which has never since been closed. He persevered with this task to such an extent that I became competent enough to do verbatim reporting, and thus transform my future, from dodgy grocer's boy to court shorthand writer, to sub-editor, to publisher. He was the first person who actually *taught* me anything, apart from Algy the bookie's runner with his detailed instruction on how not to kick a toe-ender and, of course, Alfie Littlehales, the seven-year-old gynaecologist.

I had been told things, but never *taught* things. Thus the world became a less formidable place and I realised that even if the fault-line could never be crossed, it didn't really matter. Paul Berry instilled in me a feeling of self-worth which has shaped my life ever since. This hasn't necessarily made me a better person, because I still have much to answer for, if ever there is a maker to meet, but it has justified my childhood belief about the values and activities of my Saturday-morning screen heroes. Being denied a proper education from the age of eleven proved to be an advantage, because through self-enquiry I learned things that were never taught in secondary schools. I began to realise that speaking with a regional accent was no cause for shame and that displaying ignorance actually empowers the learning process, whereas disregarding ignorance merely affirms a cycle of worthlessness.

Unbeknown to me at the time, for he was not a man to boast, Paul Berry was a long-time friend and literary executor for Vera Brittain, feminist, writer and pacifist, the author of *Testament of Youth* which ranks as one of the best autobiographical works concerning the total futility and misery of the First World War. He later became the co-author of her much-acclaimed biography. And there was I, Georgie Porter, being told by him that I had the ability to write, regardless of my lack of schooling or poor grasp of grammar.

> *"It doesn't matter, George, most of us can't but some of us can."*

So I started to read 'real' books. I began with the Iliad and spent a great deal of free time immersed in a peculiar mix of Greek tragedy and comedy, alongside Arnold Bennett, George Bernard Shaw, Dante, Yevgeny Yevtushenko, Robert Graves and many, many more poets. I began to feel, if not educated then at least literate, and able to formulate my own ideas into written words. The process has never stopped. Nevertheless, I did keep my activities quiet, especially in regard to the poetry, for had my contemporaries learned of this, my life would have become intolerable.

So, by the age of seventeen I was primed to be a man-soldier – notwithstanding my new-found independence of thought – for a further nine years and indeed, I played the game. A similar game to that I played as a child – I wasn't like them, but shared guilt by association. The first line of my report on entering man's service saying '*Porter is a first-class soldier*' was written by someone who had never met me. It was a godsend. My frailties were never once brought to the fore and my future as a warrior, serving in the illustrious RASC, was secure.